More Praise for *Your Successful Preschooler*

"The authors offer a rich integration of information from current work in brain physiology as it directly applies to the developing young child. The book is very readable and will help guide parents toward healthy choices for their preschoolers. It also suggests how to accelerate vital links between learning and socialization, critical precursors to later academic and social success."

—**Bruce Hauptman**, MD, child psychiatrist,
Cambridge, Massachusetts

"*Your Successful Preschooler* covers an impressive range of important topics while still being highly readable. It will appeal to a broad range of readers because of the artful blending of examples of real children playing and talking that are interwoven with discussion of research. There is wisdom in the discussion of the value of play because dramatic play is critically important to many facets of development and the time for play is being steadily eroded."

—**David Dickinson**, EdD; chair and professor
of teaching and learning, Peabody College,
Vanderbilt University

"*Your Successful Preschooler* is a valuable resource for parents, teachers, childcare providers, or anyone working directly with young children. Drs. Densmore and Bauman simplify the complexities of the preschool child's developing brain and provide concrete strategies for promoting the development of skills leading to young children's social and emotional competence and future academic success."

—**Jacalyn Coyne**, coordinator, Early Childhood
Education and Pathway to Teaching Careers,
Tunxis Community College

"Finally there is a book that helps parents understand the vital connection between deep engagement in play, and social and academic success. Parents who read this book will have the framework they need to navigate their children through the minefields that can derail their young children's optimal development and fulfillment in these challenging times."

—**Diane E. Levin**, PhD; professor of education, Wheelock College, Boston; author of *So Sexy So Soon* and *Remote Control Childhood*

"Bravo to Ann Densmore for recognizing that there are no issues children will confront in their lives that aren't also experienced in play. This book should be read by every early childhood curriculum specialist who believes that learning to read in preschool is more important than learning how to navigate life."

—**Marilyn V. Walsh**, head teacher, Apple Orchard School

"Parents and early childhood educators . . . will benefit from the invaluable knowledge contained in this book."

—**Kathy Wheeler**, head teacher, Cambridge-Ellis School

"Dr. Ann Densmore brings to this work a wealth of professional experience and knowledge to guide parents and professionals through the language maze. In this book, Ann demonstrates skills that can make a real difference in the lives of children. Her approach is refreshingly direct and thoughtful."

—**Nancy Fuller**, executive director and founder, Community Therapeutic Day School

Your
Successful
Preschooler

Your Successful Preschooler

Ten Skills Children Need to Become Confident and Socially Engaged

Ann Densmore, EdD
Margaret Bauman, MD

Harvard Health Publications
HARVARD MEDICAL SCHOOL
Trusted advice for a healthier life

JOSSEY-BASS
A Wiley Imprint
www.josseybass.com

Published by Jossey-Bass
A Wiley Imprint
989 Market Street, San Francisco, CA 94103-1741—www.josseybass.com

Jossey-Bass books and products are available through most bookstores. To contact Jossey-Bass directly call our Customer Care Department within the U.S. at 800-956-7739, outside the U.S. at 317-572-3986, or fax 317-572-4002.

Jossey-Bass also publishes its books in a variety of electronic formats. Some content that appears in print may not be available in electronic books.

Library of Congress Cataloging-in-Publication Data

Densmore, Ann
   Your successful preschooler : ten skills children need to become confident and socially engaged/Ann Densmore, Margaret Bauman.
       p. cm.
   Includes bibliographical references and index.
   ISBN 978-0-470-49898-9 (pbk.); ISBN 978-0-470-92585-0 (ebk);
ISBN 978-0-470-92586-7 (ebk); ISBN 978-0-470-92587-4 (ebk)
   1. Social skills in children.   2. Social interaction in children.   3. Preschool children—Psychology.   I. Bauman, Margaret.   II. Title.
   BF723.S62D46 2011
   649'.68—dc22

                                                                      2010037990

Printed in the United States of America
FIRST EDITION
PB Printing 10 9 8 7 6 5 4 3 2 1

To my late mother, Margaret Mary Walsh Densmore, who gave me laughter and love and, most important, introduced me to the world of imagination and creativity.

Ann Densmore, EdD

※

To my devoted, hardworking staff at the LADDERS clinic, whose passion and devotion to the families and children we serve each day is without parallel. They are an exceptional group of people, and I am truly honored and grateful to have them as colleagues.

Margaret Bauman, MD

Contents

Note to the Reader

THIS BOOK CONTAINS SOCIALIZATION tips and strategies that will help some children become more social and more successful in their preschool life. Even with dedicated parents, expert therapists who can engage children in play, and early intervention in preschool, some children may not necessarily make the kind of progress that we'd like to see. Some children may need attention to medical problems in order to be more receptive to the types of treatment and strategies described in this book. Parents and teachers must approach all of these strategies with caution and monitor the child's progress every day. If the child doesn't progress, perhaps another method might help the child move ahead in the socialization process. Sometimes a combination of several methods works better. Some children respond to play and to direct instruction at the same time or at different times during their preschool years. Sometimes a multifaceted approach is best. These strategies won't help all preschoolers, but they will help many.

The names and certain characteristics of the children and the schools in this book, and other identifying details when necessary, have been changed to protect confidentiality.

Acknowledgments

I THANK ALL OF THE WONDERFUL preschools, teachers, and administrators who inspired me to write this book. They have taught me the value of helping young children connect their emotions with language and the importance of play. They include the Children's Meeting House, Concord, Massachusetts, and its director, Donna Cormier, and preschool teachers Janet Craig, Linda Fox, and Chris Sabella; the Leap School, Bedford, Massachusetts, and executive director Robin Shapiro; the Apple Orchard School; the Cambridge Ellis School and particularly, Jenifer Demko, the director; the Friends School, Cambridge, Massachusetts, and particularly Beth Ann Boelter-Dimock; the Community Therapeutic Day School, Lexington, Massachusetts, especially Nancy Fuller, the director, Dr. Bruce Hauptman, psychiatrist, and Alan Shapiro, program director; the Infant Toddler Children's Center, Acton, Massachusetts; the Preschool (PAWS) program in Wellesley, Massachusetts; the Tobin School, including director Mary Beth Claus Tobin, assistant head of school Lori Davis, and teachers Lindsey Nickerson, Meghan O'Hara, and Joseph Bartholomew; Eliot Pearson Children's School, Medford, Massachusetts, particularly director Debbie Lee Keenan, assistant director Maryann O'Brien, and speech pathologist Rae Ann Somerville. I thank my associate, Lauren

Alessi, for her collaboration and wonderful work with children for Child Talk, Lexington, Massachusetts.

I particularly thank Dr. Alex Harrison, MD, for her collaboration with me and my preschoolers and their families. I'm grateful to Dr. Ned Hallowell, MD, for his encouragement and insistence that I write about my clinical work, and also Dr. Sherry Haydock, MD, of Harvard Medical School, who has given me incredible support for over twenty years, as well as Dr. David Slovik, MD, and Dr. Jesse Jupiter, MD. I thank Dr. Michael Wilson, MD, and the staff at MGH Allergy and Immunology Department of Medicine. It has been a privilege to be part of all of the lives of the wonderful dedicated people who contributed in some way to this book. I thank Dr. Julie Silver, MD, chief editor of books at Harvard Health Publications (HHP), Harvard Medical School, and Edward H. Coburn, HHP publishing director, for their patience and support during the writing process. It was an honor and a privilege to be a part of the HHP team. I thank Linda Konner, the agent for HHP, for her dedicated guidance with this project. I thank Alan Rinzler, editor for Jossey-Bass, for his support and keen sense of organization for this book and Carol Hartland for shepherding it through production. I thank Robert Kegan, my teacher and professor at Harvard Graduate School of Education, who laughed and cried with me over the children, the stories, and the ideas and who was most helpful with the basic theories underlying the method of narrative play therapy.

I thank Bruce Patton, cofounder of the Harvard Project on Negotiation, for his advice and consultation regarding negotiation, compromise, and flexibility. I'm grateful to Dr. David Dickinson, professor and chair of the Department of Teaching and Learning at Vanderbilt University, for his continued support and advice regarding young children's literacy and language.

I thank Teresa May-Benson, occupational therapist registered and licensed (OTR/L), for help with the manuscript on the subject of sensory integration and Jane Koomar, ORT/L, director, and her staff at Occupational Therapy Associates (OTA), Watertown, for their advice and wonderful work with many of the children I treat for speech and language issues. I'm grateful for the expertise of neuropsychologist Tara O'Leary, who helped with the chapter on executive function and organization for preschoolers.

I thank Dr. Jerome Kagan, Harvard psychologist, who for many years helped me understand the temperament and the neurobiology of the developing child, and Dr. Torkel Klingberg, MD, for his conversation at the MIT conference on the concepts of brain plasticity and neurobiology of the brain, which provided key information for our book.

I thank a special group of colleagues and friends who provided creative ideas and support for this book: Phyl Solomon, Sandra Farrar, Susan Zorb, Arlene McNulty, Joanne Berger, Jacquie Kay, Mary Jeka, Ute Lutjens, Beth Dionne, Daniel Reinstein, Olivia von Ferstel, and Bridget Glenshaw. I thank my colleagues and friends Joan Axelrod, Jed Lehrich, Molly Smith, Steve Lessin, Roberta Hodson, Mary Coakley-Welch, Jenice Ely, Dr. Janice Ware, Sarah Measures, Karen Levine, Naomi Chedd, Lauren Weeks, Dr. James Magauran, MD, Ann Helmus, and many others. I thank the people who encouraged me to keep going: Sharon Hogan; Marjorie Gatchell; Gunnel Schmidt; Diane and Peter Gray; Carol Burt; Rachel Bulbulian; Claudia Kronenberg; Judy Raleigh; Merrily Bishop; Rebecca Kahler-Reis and her children, Jakob, Anna, and Jennifer; Jean Ayers; Betsy Janzen; Sara Serisky; Regina Pacor; Brit Iliff; Elaine Duggan; and Laura Simonian.

I thank Pam Liflander, writer and author, for her dedication, patience, and skill that helped me create this book. I couldn't have finished the book without her expertise. I thank Barbara Smith, consultant to Child Talk, editor, and parent, who gave me ideas and editing advice. I thank Bev Miller, copyeditor for this book, for her insight. I also thank my legal counsel, Bill Strong, Esquire, for his support and advice. I'm grateful for Russ Campbell who provided dedicated technical support.

I thank my wonderful daughters, Dr. Kristin Bennett and Jennifer Bennett, for their love and support and, most of all, for being part of my life. I thank my cousin Jim Antonioli for his continued support and expertise on writing well; my brother John Densmore for his encouragement; and my cousin Maryann Kleinman for her devoted support.

At last, I thank all the many families and children I have known over the past thirty years who were devoted and dedicated to being a part of the team. With the families' hard work and loving support, these children made progress, and I am deeply grateful for the privilege of working in my clinical practice with all of them.

Ann Densmore, EdD

§

I thank my late husband, Dr. Roger A. Bauman, and our three children, all of whom have been involved and supportive of my work in autism. I am deeply grateful to my longtime friend, mentor, and research colleague, Dr. Thomas L. Kemper, without whose help and influence my research career would have been impossible. I also thank the many families who, over more than forty years, have entrusted the care of their children to me and to our clinical practice. Many of us have laughed and cried together, and it has been a privilege to have been a part of their lives.

Margaret Bauman, MD

Your
Successful
Preschooler

Introduction

OVER THE PAST THIRTY YEARS, we have diagnosed and treated thousands of children with all kinds of learning issues. Many of these children come to us with a combination of medical, emotional, and developmental problems, yet their parents are also asking us to evaluate their children's social performance. Specifically, parents want to know if learning and socialization are linked.

We see parents who agonize over whether their child will make friends. They want to know if social skills can be taught, like reading or math, or if these skills will develop naturally. As one parent said, "My preschooler can talk, take turns, and be polite, but other children don't gravitate to him. He's a loner. I just don't know why."

Every day we see preschoolers who can play, run, and talk on playgrounds and in classrooms. Yet these same children don't know how to connect with others and make friends, even though their teachers describe them as typical children. It is very clear to us that some children retreat from others and don't make social connections, while others are more gregarious and seem to be the ones who become leaders and well-liked children.

As a speech and language pathologist (Ann) and a pediatric neurologist (Margaret), we know that all parents wants to make sure that their children are happy, well adjusted, and social. Parents also want to know exactly how their children should behave, how they are supposed to relate with their friends for each of the preschool developmental milestones, and what their role should be to ensure that their children succeed in all aspects of life. They're looking for ways to counter the violence children are exposed to in the media; they want their children to be just as happy when they are unplugged from video games and television as they are when they are connected.

Most important, parents want to make sure that their children are liked by others. Parents and teachers constantly ask us, "How can I get my preschooler to fully engage with the others in the classroom?" or, "How will my child develop strong relationships and lifelong friendships?"

At the same time, parents and teachers are increasingly concerned about real academic pressures: today's children are asked to do more in school and to do it earlier than previous generations. Although most parents know that there needs to be time for play and socialization during the preschool day, most are aware of federally mandated testing requirements through No Child Left Behind or specific testing required for admission into the best public and private schools. These pressures can drive parents and teachers to value academics before play, even though studies have consistently shown that this is not the best model for preschool education.

These are some of the issues that we address in this book. Our goal is to give parents and teachers the tools they need to help preschool children prepare for academic achievement and become more socially connected. As parents, you can help your child become successful. And just as important, your child needs to be in a preschool environment that focuses on play that facilitates social interactions and relationships.

We are aware of the stress today's parents face. Parents are under enormous pressure to be the "best," and new and often conflicting research is readily available to them. We also know that some families have fewer resources than others or may not be geographically located near formal preschool programs. Nevertheless, the suggestions in this book can work in any preschool or day care environment where the teachers are open to making changes, and they can be implemented right at home too.

SCIENTIFIC BREAKTHROUGHS THAT AFFECT PARENTING

A 2008 joint study from the University of British Columbia and the Sackler Institute at Weill/Cornell Medical College has shown that the brain is more plastic, or able to change, than previously thought. These scientists state, "One major contribution of neuroscience to understanding cognitive development has been in demonstrating that biology is not destiny—that is, demonstrating the remarkable role of experience in shaping the mind, the brain, and body."[1] In another 2008 study, reported by the National Scientific Council on the Developing Child through Harvard University, investigators found that experiences specifically gained during this sensitive period of the preschool years play an exceptionally important role in the capacities of the brain.[2] This research suggests that the developing brain is most plastic between the ages of three and five years, a sensitive period that coincides with the preschool years. The brain architecture is build over a succession of what are referred to as "sensitive periods" that develop more circuits and more complex skills. Early experience is important for the probability of positive outcomes. Thus, we know that the period of time when parents and teachers can affect the greatest change is during the preschool years. At this critical juncture, children are best able to learn how to socialize, learn moral behavior, and develop empathy, altruism, cooperation, negotiation, and even leadership.

Our own experience, coupled with these studies, points to preschool as one of the most formative periods in child development. A 2007 report from the U.S. Department of Education's National Center for Education Statistics documented that 57 percent of American children ages three to five attended center-based programs: day care, Head Start programs, preschools, and early prekindergarten programs. These children attended preschool for at least one year before kindergarten.[3] Studies have previously shown that these children have a distinct academic advantage in both language and math skills over those who don't attend preschool, regardless of their socioeconomic backgrounds. Alphabet songs, puzzles, and math games help preschoolers mature into higher-achieving children as long as their preschool day also includes several hours of the most important aspect: socialization. Researchers agree that because there appears to be a clear link between play and brain development during this critically important time frame, children who have attended preschool appear to achieve higher academic scores than those who have not attended preschool and may become more emotionally well adjusted by the third grade.

PRESCHOOL ISN'T ENOUGH

Facilitating peer interaction is a challenging job because each child is unique. Each teacher or parent also has a unique history and culture that often dictates how each relates to his or her children at school and at home. What each child needs stems from his or her own cultural values, biology, and family history.

As parents and teachers, we need to see these differences and cultivate social experiences that respect each child. Some families value storytelling at the dinner table, and others may value a child's adherence to quieter rules. Some parents may want their child to be home-schooled, other parents want their child to learn from the surrounding world, and still others want them to learn from texts or more adult-directed experiences. Some children have hunger, loneliness, and pain in their environment. And some experience trauma or deprivation.

As teachers, we need to respect and comprehend the many differences in family conversations and social cues—facial expression, body language, and tone of voice. We know there are many differences in family belief systems and values that affect each child's life. We need to see each child in the preschool setting as unique and give them respect and a sense of community. As teachers we also need to understand our own family histories, how we talk to our own children, and how our parents talked to us. Our own culture influences how we perceive the children we are trying to help.

We believe that children are born with certain abilities but that they can learn from their environment through such experiences as play and social interactions with peers. A helpful preschool, a day care program, or a home school setting is where a child can learn to be social, build confidence, develop a sense of moral character, learn how to negotiate with peers, and succeed in social situations with peers.

Although it may not always be possible for teachers to closely observe children with peers during choice time or at recess in preschool, our experience suggests that much of the time, some children may not be really interacting with each other and may need help to do so.

Children may look as if they are engaged, but they may be just following each other. The play yard is filled with children climbing, running, jumping, and screaming. A few preschoolers are climbing together. Another group is digging in the sandbox, but only a few of the children are looking at each other. Still another group may be playing tag without rules, racing around the playground without a clear purpose. When the preschoolers move inside into the classroom, the norm is "structure" or "free play," with some guidance by teachers. During center time, children have some chance to talk to each other and share special objects. In some preschools, center time is an opportunity for teaching social pragmatic skills, that is, turn taking, how to enter and exit a conversation, how to stay on a topic, and how to make comments to others. During this time, some teachers teach such skills as an example of the importance of showing empathy for others, how to become a kind person, and how to respect others.

Despite their best efforts, however, it's not possible for teachers to facilitate language and social interaction for every class member who needs help. Many preschool teachers want extra guidance so that they can encourage more social conversation skills in their classroom. Even the best preschool teachers, those who allow long periods of play during the day, still ask for advice on how to teach better skills for negotiation and problem solving. The best preschool teachers know that the most important part of the preschool experience is the social component: interaction with peers and acceptance by them, which is directly associated with higher levels of functioning throughout school and in later life.

The fact is that the most socially successful children do better throughout every developmental stage for these reasons:

- They tend to be well rounded and emotionally stable.
- They easily make the transition to elementary school with confidence due to their increased self-esteem and ability to communicate their own ideas.
- They are more likely to achieve in most academic subjects. Children who are connected to peers socially in preschool are better achievers and read faster by the third grade.
- They create connections to both teachers and other students. These relationships are essential to becoming a friendly, content child and a socially adjusted adult.

THE TEN SKILLS THAT ENCOURAGE SOCIALLY SUCCESSFUL PRESCHOOLERS

We have found that the most successful preschoolers acquire ten unique skills. Children with these skills often attract and maintain friendships, which allow them to socialize throughout the day. These children are:

1. *Likable.* They can build long-term, meaningful friendships. They know how to play with more than one child, positively reinforce their friends when they succeed, recognize and acknowledge a peer who is sad or disappointed, and use a play date to make a real connection.

2. *Achieving.* They achieve complex language skills, which will lead to later academic achievement. They can use appropriate vocabulary, experience success as well as defeat with grace, and adjust their focus if an agenda changes.

3. *Happy.* They are optimistic and confident, and they have a sense of self. They understand the perspective of other children; interpret their peer's gestures, facial expressions, and body language; and speak and listen attentively to others.

4. *Of strong moral character.* They have the ability to form attachments to the ideals of a larger community rather than themselves, for the good of others. They understand what is right or wrong during difficult play situations, which will increase their awareness of when they need adults to help.

5. *Resilient.* They can tap into the most effective coping skills that allow them to handle disappointment, manage a crisis, and seek positive attributes in play situations. These children can bounce back easily and regroup when they face stressful situations.

6. *Flexible.* They can allow others to change the agenda of play and develop their own ideas within an interaction. They can listen to the perspective of others and achieve compromise when necessary. When sudden problems arise in play, they can find options and redirect themselves and others to help the situation. They accept surprises and adjust easily to change.

7. *Organized.* They can use logical reasoning and organizational skills, which will foster academic achievement and a sense of capability. These children can develop stories in play. They assign roles and follow a sequence of actions as they play. They respect others' culture and agree to follow other ways of constructing stories as long as they are formed with clear ideas.

8. *Leaders.* They can assume a leadership role within a group with both humility and positive self-esteem without acting like bullies. They can ask a group of peers to play a game and help each child engage. They have a sense of humor when things don't work out and are the first to forgive a friend who makes a mistake or doesn't

follow the rules of the game. They keep the group cohesive and enthusiastic about their social connection and play.

9. *Socially engaged.* They can show enthusiasm by being present, alert, and aware when engaging with their friends. They pay attention to others, know what their friends are thinking, and are able to show their friends that they are being heard. They give the group a sense of cohesiveness and a feeling of belonging.

10. *Passionate about learning.* They have a noticeable sense of curiosity and creativity and a wide variety of interests. These children are interested in the world around them and can convey their knowledge to others. They love to investigate, construct projects, and motivate others to do the same.

Many, if not most, children fall somewhere on the continuum of mastering these skills, and over time, they achieve some level of competency. Children who have more challenges—those with learning issues, behavioral issues, or developmental issues—may have a harder time acquiring these skills. The main goal of parenting should be never to give up trying to help your child.

In order to assist their development, we have created specific strategies for teaching children how to be more social. Through this process, we have found that these same strategies can help children acquire these skills. And we predict that this early intervention in mastering these skills during a period of rapid brain development will help many children become more successful.

ABOUT THIS BOOK

The program that we have created defines a useful and practical means of talking to children that will help them become socially engaged for life. We aim to give parents, teachers, and other caregivers the specific strategies they need to provide the most effective experiences that can affect the developing brain. By reading this book, they will be able to help young children develop the effective ways to engage their friends, making social interactions easier and more meaningful.

Chapter One offers an introduction to the brain and how it acquires new information and learned behaviors. Then we provide helpful tips for reviewing and defining a preschool that is in line with our philosophy and show how to incorporate useful strategies into any preschool setting, home school, or day care situation.

Each of the following chapters discusses the ten traits that successful children share and strategies for developing these traits. Each of the strategies is geared to the achievement of specific results. For example, being a likable child requires building friendships. Being an advanced child requires understanding complex language.

These core strategies have been developed based on Dr. Ann Densmore's theory of narrative play. Both of us have been collaborating for over twenty years about children with disabilities. Dr. Margaret Bauman evaluates and diagnoses children who would benefit from treatment using a variety of techniques discussed in this book. Narrative play incorporates speech therapy with peer relationships in natural settings. For years Ann has helped children engage socially by combining language, play, and narrative or storytelling. This developmental play-based approach to socialization can help your child learn how to engage with other children, as well as with adults, at a meaningful level.

Each strategy is supported by dialogue from actual preschoolers who have learned to engage and sustain friendships, increasing their own social skills. According to current research, preschoolers who engage in socialization will gain self-confidence by using language for negotiating and increase their academic achievement in kindergarten and the primary grades.

Many parents who have followed this program have told us that they were able to see their child in a totally different light and were able to deepen their own relationships with them. They were thrilled to experience their child's joy in forming friendships that can last a lifetime.

CHAPTER ONE

Children Can Learn to Be Successful

AS ADULTS, WE STRIVE to learn something new every day. Yet the youngest children can accomplish the same task almost without trying. In no other time of life can we literally see learning occur right before our eyes. We're transfixed as an infant suddenly crawls at seven months and then can walk just a few months later. A child's babbling at six months may become expressive speech in just a year.

This chapter introduces the basic developmental signs of a typical child in moving from toddlerhood toward preschool years, including the changes of the developing brain. Parents and teachers need to have some baseline reference to help them observe how their child is developing and learning to become more successful as a person.

- By *success*, we don't mean that your child is destined to graduate from Harvard Law School at the age of sixteen. Instead, we mean that a child is resourceful, confident, and happy and gives to the wider community. It's a long road toward this success, but it begins early in a child's life.

Babies, even those who still can't walk or talk, begin to engage in pretend play as young as eighteen months.[1] A toddler can pretend to comb a doll's hair with a pencil or wave a stick as if it were a magic wand, giggling as she plays to show that she knows she's pretending. Research shows that two and three year olds giggle when they pretend play so we won't take them too seriously. Soon even the youngest preschoolers are turning objects like blocks into fire engines as they shove them along the floor. They create simple stories and can describe their worlds—both the real one and the fantasy world of play.

We know that children who can understand and see the perspective of others and interpret what other children are thinking will become more successful. And we can see this development happen in just the same way as we witness our children learning to walk and talk. First they explore their options, and later they become more aware of others. When this occurs, children can begin to create real relationships within their family.

As children are exposed to empathy, moral behavior, and control of their emotions and behavior, they are learning the skills that will allow them to become increasingly social. They practice and learn as they pretend play with their friends and mimic the actions of their parents and teachers. Even as preschoolers, children begin to view the world and report back to us exactly what they see, how they feel, and what they think. As they master each of these developmental milestones and face new social experiences, the structure and function of their brain is altered, becoming more integrated and more efficient.

UNDERSTANDING CHILDREN THROUGH NEUROSCIENCE

Functional magnetic resonance imaging (fMRI) is a technology that allows us to observe the complexity of the brain activity as it handles and processes different types of information. Research utilizing fMRI studies is dramatically changing the way we understand the brain. For example, we now know that when we're writing or talking, the brain is engaged and "lights up" in several areas, where we previously thought that only one distinct area of the brain was involved in that particular activity. At the present time, the vast majority of this research has been performed on adults because of the high degree of cooperation required on the part of the research subject. Thus, much of the information we now have about the brain function comes largely from adult studies and can only be extrapolated for helping us to understand how the child's brain develops.

Nevertheless, we do know that every human brain is vulnerable to change because it has some degree of *plasticity*, that is, the ability to modify and grow both structurally and functionally. Previously it was thought that the brain was limited in its capacity to change. Formerly, scientists and other medical researchers believed that any change in brain structure was purely biological and that the brain stopped developing once an individual reached adulthood. Today we know that the interactions between our biology and our experience can help modify and shape our brain structure. Specific experiences and interventions can directly and positively affect the neuronal connections in our brain. This growth can occur at any time. These changes can occur at any time through a mechanism—*neurogenesis*—the process through which new brain cells may develop and create new pathways. Some of these circuits affect intelligence and attention throughout life. Neuroscientist Torkel Klingberg discussed brain plasticity at a recent conference at MIT, where he stated, "What scientists have found is that rather than [the brain] being static, this map is forever being redrawn."[2]

One of the greatest windows of opportunity for this type of development occurs during the preschool years. In order to take advantage of this critical time for learning, parents, caregivers, and teachers first need to understand how the brain works.

A PRIMER ON THE BRAIN

Every brain is composed of several billion brain cells, called *neurons*, and trillions of connections, or *synapses*, that help relay electrical messages sent by these neurons throughout the brain and the body. These electrical messages are carried by brain chemicals called *neurotransmitters*. Brain development is measured in many ways, including monitoring levels of neurotransmitter production, as well as identifying an increase in the number of neuronal connections. New connections are made with every learned behavior or stored critical fact. As these neuronal connections increase, the brain literally grows in size and weight.

Brain development is actually a perfect example of the motto, "Use it or lose it." The large mass of neurons present in an infant's brain is waiting to be programmed into synaptic connections. Some connections, like breathing, are preprogrammed. However, the vast majority are learned and developed. During the first ten years of life, the brain is supersaturated with neurons waiting for learned behaviors to present themselves in order to become synapses.

By the age of two years, a child's synaptic density begins to gradually decrease through a process referred to as *pruning*: important connections are becoming reinforced, while other less important ones die back improving the efficiency of the brain. Even with all this pruning, a typical three year old still has nearly 1,000 trillion synapses, which is twice the number of an adult brain, making his brain two and a half times more active than an adult's.[3]

The late psychologist Myrtle McGraw's research on child development identified and described the concept of critical periods of learning, developmental windows during which children suddenly reach a period of rapid development and can demonstrate new abilities in many different areas. One of these critical periods falls between the ages of three and five years. Scientists now believe that this same period occurs at a time of high brain plasticity: when the brain is subject to accepting change in neuronal development. The earliest experiences of children, primarily in the first five years of life, play a critical role in determining the ultimate wiring of the brain: how many synaptic connections remain into adulthood. The greater the number of selected neuronal connections, the greater the complexity of the brain, which then has implications for each child's social, creative, and intellectual abilities. This is why it is so important to capture and take advantage of this critically important window.

As children grow older, the number of potential synapses begins to decline—so much so that by late adolescence, about half of the brain's synapses have been discarded. If connections are not made, the neurons simply die off. The existing connections that have been made may be reinforced, or *crystallized*, into habitual behaviors. This means that if a child has developed a particular negative behavior, such as acting out or ignoring other children, and it is not corrected early, it may be more difficult to change later.

Our goal then is to make the most of this critical time of brain plasticity, so that we can ensure that we imprint positive behaviors that will lead to success for children. Parents and teachers can now be assured that intervention—whether it is play therapy, relationship-based therapy, behavioral therapy, or a combination of several methods—does work. Your child may respond to any and all of these methods. In some cases, children can learn to act and learn differently. A shy child does not have to remain a shy child, and an aggressive child is not destined for a life of violence. Although we can't guarantee that a particular therapy or intervention or approach will change a particular circuitry of the brain, we can say, as Torkel Klingberg writes, that "all types of experience and learning modify the brain." When we modify our brain, we can change our life.[4]

HOW LEARNING HAPPENS

Children acquire new information and behaviors in a variety of ways, but we believe that socialization is one of the most important paths to rapid learning. In order to maximize brain development, children need constant exposure to people and experiences. And interestingly, we've found that children think best, learn best, and socialize best when their work and their play relate to their peers and the world in which they live. As a parent, your job is to facilitate the right types of learning, in the right environments.

That infants learn by observing is well documented. A baby who is watching his mother may be waving his hand and cooing. If his mother waves her hand back, smiles, and makes the same sounds, the baby may repeat the same gesture and song. This is called a *reciprocal interaction*. The baby will remember this exchange, and if it is pleasurable, he will try to get his mother to do it again.

Preschool children continue to learn in the same manner: through engagement with their family, teachers and caregivers, and peers. In the midst of interaction, they are increasing their vocabulary by listening to the different ways that words and ideas are shared. They're also learning the skills they need to become social.

Constant interaction also gives children the opportunity to learn through imitation. An infant tries to mimic the sounds of his mother, siblings, or even the bird outside his window. A toddler wants to copy his big brother and tries to eat dinner with a spoon, even if the cereal never makes it to his mouth. A preschooler will strive to imitate his friends and play the same games and use the same words in their constant banter on the playground. There is good reason that younger siblings understand how to negotiate better than their older brothers and sisters: they have been listening to family interactions. They can imitate the same behavior and, if they want, get the same results.

Preschoolers can learn by creating their own variations on what they think, hear, and see. They may listen to their older brother's argument with Mom and realize that this behavior isn't getting the right results. In the future, the younger sibling might take a different tack to get a desired result. Young children also learn by experimenting with language and trying out interactions. They find new options for using new words and create new ideas as they socially engage.

The brain also changes and develops when we expose it to excessive activation—when we regularly practice at something, such as playing a musical instrument or mastering a particular motor skill. Children need to practice to be able to hold on to new ideas, use their working memory, and develop short-term or long-term memory and problem-solving skills. They can learn how to be empathic by first listening to an adult and then by practicing these same exchanges with their friends.

Practice doesn't always guarantee success. Sometimes no matter how much you practice classical guitar, you might not be able to master the nuances of the music. Some children are inherently better at some tasks than others. However, most children need adult guidance in order to attain even the most basic level of proficiency.

We support the idea of preschool, although we know that children can develop and grow without this formal structure. Some parents choose to keep their child at home. For them, there are other ways for children to socialize, including after-school groups, play groups, sport activities, cooperative play situations with other parents and children, and time with their family at home, particularly with daily contact with siblings.

THE RIGHT PRESCHOOL MATTERS

In a perfect world, parents and caregivers would have plenty of time to spend with their children and meet all of their physical, social, and intellectual needs. But with our busy schedules, siblings to care for, and other adult distractions, parents and even caregivers have difficulty being present for their children, especially when it comes to creating the optimum social environment for success and learning. That's why we believe that one way for children to learn new behaviors between the ages of three and five years is in a preschool program with play, outside time, art, daily storybook reading, and creative activities developed through books and curriculum that are systematic, but incorporates play that enriches children's language. We hope children at this age will have wonderful teachers who can encourage peer interactions, and a strong bond of communication with the child's family. We encourage preschools to develop units and ongoing themes that change throughout the year that give a child immersion into new ideas and worlds through play and activity-based learning—engagement in play with materials, props, and ideas that encourage language and learning. This should happen in preschools on a daily basis.

Our definition of *preschool* is relatively broad. For the purposes of this book, we are including half-day and full-day programs, day care centers, private and public preschools, and also home schooling. Preschools vary in how they accept children. Some preschools accept children who have special needs and others accept children with particular talents such as in sports, artistic skills, or with academic potential. Some preschools accept children without any restrictions and don't interview the child. Preschools also vary in their length of day. Some begin as a three-hour class and eventually lead to a five-hour or a full day that includes an after-school program. Some children are in preschool five days a week; others are in class three mornings or afternoons a week, or two mornings a week for three hours a day. Parents need to consider the length of their child's day and whether she can manage the number of hours she's in school. Some preschools, in some parts of the world, are schools without supplies except for the environment and handmade tools. Some preschool-aged children have no school at all. They learn from their siblings and their family unit. Some children can only hope to survive and a formal education is not a part of their life.

Not every preschool will work for your child. Some preschools are better managed, and better funded, than others. And to make things more complicated, parents have been fed a decade's worth of mixed messages in this country. In this country, as well as others, today's parents are often caught in the middle of conflicting claims from experts: on one hand, they know children must have time to play; on the other hand, they are anxious about the competition to get their child into the right elementary schools in order to stay on track for the best high schools and colleges. Many parents don't have a choice of what public elementary school their child will be assigned to and whether or not they can request a particular school. And they are aware of the pressure of standardized testing in elementary school, a fear that drives many preschools toward an academic curriculum. Many parents are specifically looking for preschools that emphasize a more academic curriculum as early as age two years.

Susan Engel, a senior lecturer in psychology and director of the teaching program at Williams College, believes, as we do, that testing requirements in preschool can be "at odds with what scientists understand about how children develop." In an opinion piece for the *New York Times*, Engel wrote, "It takes time and guidance to learn how to get along, to listen to one another and to cooperate. These skills can't be picked up casually at the corners of the day."[5]

This type of test-driven education is often not age appropriate for the preschool child, and it encourages a hurried approach to learning. Research shows that when preschool children spend too much time on worksheets rather than play-based or activity-based learning, they become restless and inattentive, and express doubt in their abilities. What's more, they are less advanced in motor, academic, language, and social skills by the end of the school year.[6] By third grade, these same children were found to have poor study habits, poor academic achievement, and increased distractibility.

However, even children who benefit from an academic preschool environment still need free, unscheduled time for creative growth, self-reflection, and decompression and would profit from the unique developmental benefits of free time and play. That is why we, along with the American Academy for Pediatrics, suggest that child care and early education programs should offer more than academic preparedness.

So how do parents choose the best preschool programs? The following sections address this question.

The Best Preschools Focus on Socialization

Our first recommendation is to choose a program that focuses on socialization, because socialization inspires learning, which is critical for healthy brain development. In most preschools, socialization is created through play and activity-based learning.

Play in and of itself is also critical for brain development. The American Academy of Pediatrics believes that play is essential to development because it contributes to the cognitive, physical, social, and emotional well-being of children and youth. It allows children to use their creativity while developing their imagination, dexterity, and physical, cognitive, and emotional strength.

Play is not always the priority of many preschools. Many preschools are limiting play in the curriculum in order to make more time for academic lessons. We do not believe that this type of curriculum is in the typical child's best interests.

In our experience, the best preschools allow children to learn how to construct projects in play with others, how to problem-solve with guidance, how to evaluate situations with critical thinking, how to see others' perspectives, and how to exchange ideas in a conversation. In short, they incorporate academic subjects in the context of group or peer interactions. As Engel writes, "Saying the alphabet does not necessarily help children learn to read. But having extended and complex conversations in toddlerhood (and in preschool) does."

Preschool Play Sets the Stage for Socialization

We believe that the best way to ensure that a child will become socially and emotionally well adjusted is by allowing her to engage in play, in addition to the classroom curriculum that is based on play and activity-based themes and storybook reading. Socially and emotionally adjusted children are able to adapt to any change in the schedule or any unpredictable moment. They can accept things as they are and move on to new projects and ideas when necessary. They also seek out social relationships with peers and classmates. They love to talk about what they are doing or making or thinking about. They enjoy being alone at times, but they prefer to be with others. They understand how others feel and think. They can negotiate and still keep a friend.

Playtime promotes a child who is happy and content. It slows the fast pace of life and allows exploration. What's more, play is one of the easiest ways to develop true friendships, one of the most significant ways to gauge whether children are socially successful.

The Importance of Dramatic Play

Preschool children can be socially engaged in many forms of play, but one of the easiest methods to ensure socialization is for preschool teachers to encourage and emphasize dramatic play. Dramatic play is the foundation of intellectual exploration, creativity, school success, curiosity, and general learning. It's how children learn problem solving, reasoning, literacy, and social skills, including cooperation and sharing.

Dramatic play is one area that seamlessly connects the academic needs of parents with the socialization skills that most preschool teachers are trained to provide. A preschool dramatic play area can be loaded with all kinds of literacy opportunities, including vocabulary, conversation, and even the earliest precursors to writing and spelling. Teachers can focus on the sequencing of ideas and the organization of thoughts. They can add to the story or help children form a complete narrative with a beginning, middle, and an end. Research has shown a direct association between dramatic and fantasy play and achievement in third grade.[7]

The features of make-believe play are perfect for stimulating changes in the cerebral cortex that underlie the development of self-regulation.[8] Dramatic play that is facilitated by an adult helps impulsive preschoolers follow directions, find their own ideas, and then play with more organization. When children engage in dramatic, make-believe play, they experience what scientists call *experience-expectant growth*. Because dramatic play includes rich social engagement with peers that is in line with the child's interests, the brain responds, and the child becomes more in control of play. This brain development results from the exploration of the environment and from having make-believe play opportunities to communicate, which is exactly the type of learning that prepares the brain for later focused learning in school.[9]

Dramatic play is also one of the foundations of self-reflection and psychological adjustment.[10] In dramatic play, a child can take on a role or idea that he may want to work through. He can see how the reactions in that role influence or even upset peers. This knowledge provides ways to reflect on what he is doing in his own, real life.

Dramatic play allows teachers to infuse academic curriculum into a play setting. One preschool that Ann often visits has an old train car sitting in a meadow. When the children approach the car, Marilyn Walsh, the teacher, talks about different places they are pretending to visit and what they'll see. As a result of that, they want to know more and more, including the names of places and where they're located.

Equally important is the fact that dramatic play fosters teamwork and community. Ann was once working with a group of preschoolers when they started a unit on space. One boy's suggestion that they make an observatory and use empty paper towel tubes as telescopes was the springboard for the learning that followed. The entire class became involved, and they learned about outer space while they played. The bonus was the great sense of community that the play created when all the children worked on the project together.

HOW TO CHOOSE THE BEST PRESCHOOL

Excellent preschools exist across the country and offer perfect settings for children to become successful and creative and develop a true passion for learning. A good preschool needs teachers who have an educational background that emphasizes clinical training and experience working with young children. Helpful and experienced teachers interact in a positive way with young children, and know how to encourage play. The length of time that the teachers have been at a particular school can be a factor in choosing a school where the teaching staff is happy and remains at the school.

Another factor to consider is whether its philosophy resonates with your own ideas. Parents must listen to their gut feeling when they enter a preschool and listen to the teachers and the children interact. Parents need to review preschools by looking at materials, books, props, and activities that are developmentally appropriate.

In order to find these schools, parents have to ask tough questions of administrators and teachers. When you attend a preschool visit, use the opportunity to determine whether the setting attends to the social and emotional developmental needs of the children and how the preschool day is created to include time for play and social interactions.

The Twelve Most Important Questions to Ask About Preschools

We tell the parents we work with to ask the following twelve questions if they are seeking the ideal standard in a preschool when they are visiting potential preschools for their child.

1. How much time is devoted to play?

In our opinion, the youngest children need at least two or three hours a day to play, preferably in a preschool environment or a well-developed home program. Play can be unstructured time or time that is guided by the teacher who creates themes and helps children tell stories as they play. The time allotted during the course of a preschool day will change depending on the length of the program. Typically an all-day program should be able to meet this requirement.

2. Do you allow parents to occasionally observe how their child is doing?

Preschool classrooms should have nothing to hide. Parents can quickly identify whether their child is successfully interacting with peers or participating in class. Allowing parents in the classroom leads to open and honest communication between the parents and the teachers, which is critical for a successful preschool experience.

The best preschools also offer opportunities for parents and teachers to get together without children present in order to discuss development and any other issues that may be arising in the classroom. This meeting should occur about every two months.

Teachers should also give parents clear instructions on the best ways to communicate with teachers and the school. When they enter a classroom, parents need to respect the teacher's priority, which is teaching and helping children. Meetings with parents and teachers need to be outside class time. The worst time for parents to talk with a teacher is during the transition in the morning when they come in, in the car pool line, or during the transition out of the classroom. Most preschools have conference days when the children are at home and the parents come in by appointment. Teachers should be ready to visit a child's home if the parent is unable to come to school to communicate about their child's ongoing progress.

3. What is a typical schedule for the day?

We believe that even in preschool or a home program, teachers need an organized curriculum with focused themes that change throughout the year. What's more, children need to be presented every day with an overriding plan for that day. A typical preschool day has the following components:

§

o   *Circle time*, which allows for children to develop a sense of community with their classmates. They typically sit in a group and learn about the weather for the day and what some children did that week. They share ideas with each other. They talk about particular subjects that help develop moral character and kindness in others. They talk about world events when needed through daily storybook reading and discussion about ideas. They learn about the class schedule for the day and who may be visiting. Circle time offers an opportunity for the children to come together to discuss whatever is on their mind or a specific lesson the teacher has prepared.

o   *Center time*, structured around different spaces in the classroom and activities that occur in those areas. Preschoolers love to move around centers that focus on creative materials. Some centers may include a "science" area with, for example, various bottles of different colored water, a selection of rocks and crystals, or a collection of shells and sea animals. Blocks are another popular center with children. They also love to have cars and trucks, front loaders, and train tracks. Other centers that are appropriate for preschoolers include a house corner or a dress-up corner with lots of hats and clothes that fit their size. They love to dress up and play different roles or create birthday parties or set a table for lunch. This area encourages dramatic play.

o   *Free time or choice time*, to allow children an opportunity to explore the classroom, finish a project, or be with their friends. Children should be able to choose if they want to return to centers, sit quietly near the book corner, or go outside (if there is enough staffing to monitor children both indoors and outdoors at the same time).

4. Does the program incorporate distinct time for music and art?

We feel that a preschool day or week should encompass music and creative arts. Music allows a child to practice rhythm, sounds, and phonology. They learn to communicate with music, dance, and song. Creative arts are essential because preschoolers learn to write or draw their ideas, which improves literacy skills as well as narrative skills. Some schools hire music and art therapists who visit the classroom each week. These consultants can support the teacher and help many children through these creative experiences.

5. Do the children have outside time every day on safe structures?

The outdoors offers extraordinary opportunities for imaginative play, a chance to communicate with peers, and an increased sense of awareness when they become a part of the natural environment. Children also need to run around and release some of the energy they have built up in the classroom. When they are allowed to do this, they'll be ready for inside classroom time.

Playground structures should be made of materials that are nontoxic and do well in all kinds of weather. They should include long tube slides, sandboxes (and lots of sand materials like shovels, buckets, and sifters), small swings, bars to hang on that are not too high, and simple climbing structures. Recently Ann was visiting a preschool that had fifteen pretend plastic lawn mowers with small pebbles inside them that made a sound like a lawn mower. The children loved to play with these as they all raced around the playground, talking to each other and laughing.

The playground needs to have surfaces that are installed according to safety standards of a play surface set up by the New York Department of Conservation (DEC) and the Department of Health who do scientific studies on playground equipment and safety. At this age, children fall when they play on structures. The new playground surfaces are made out of pressed rubber and other nontoxic materials with low-dust content that meet certain critical standards. The playground flooring is also a place to race cars or use objects outside in play. Playgrounds need lots of balls, sponge bats, and things to throw back and forth like a Frisbee. Not all schools will have the funding to provide these special surfaces for the playground.

Parents should be informed as to what types of clothing children need for outdoor play. If the class is planning to go sledding on a snowy day, the children need snow pants, boots, hats, and mittens. In hot weather, children need water shoes, bathing suits, and a towel. Some preschools may need to provide clothing for children who don't have several changes of clothes, boots, or shoes.

6. How much time is allotted for dramatic play?

A good program has to include time for children to engage in make-believe, at least during choice time each day. Dramatic play should not be limited to girls' dress-up or make-believe. Children want to explore all sorts of adult roles. They can create a storefront, and the teachers can focus on math, with lessons on how much they should charge for things, decision making (which purchases to make, which to pass by), and more.

In one preschool class, the teachers were talking about different professions, including doctors, and one child suggested that they create a doctor's office. The teachers brought in a stethoscope and carried up some old white tables from the school basement. A parent brought in some old x-rays and a pretend doctor set. Another mother, who was a doctor, came in and talked to the children about her job. She answered lots of questions and let the children see what it looked like when a doctor peeked into ears. After that, the kids decided to turn the lower loft into the waiting room, complete with receptionist, and the upper loft into the operating room. It was a busy place, full of conversation and rich vocabulary. The children were happy to learn the names of all the instruments.

7. What type of sensory experiences does the classroom provide?

Preschoolers should have plenty of sensory-type activities, such as a water table or access to sand or clay. Many preschoolers have the need for "deep pressure," that is, the need to dive under a beanbag or a cushion and cover up with blankets. Other children need to bounce on a small trampoline or swing to relieve stress. Some may want small objects to fidget with during times when they feel the need. Occupational therapists can design preschool activities in any school that incorporates these sensory experiences, so ask if the preschool you are investigating has a relationship with this kind of therapist.

8. Do you have a parent group or meetings for parents to attend for information about raising a preschooler?

Group meetings can help parents learn from each other and develop a sense of school community. Parents need access to ideas and options when they are raising a typical preschooler, and they need support from other parents who are facing the same challenges.

9. What is the ratio between children and teachers in each classroom?

The lower the teacher-child ratio, the more time an adult will have to give children individual attention when they need help negotiating or chatting with classmates. They will also have more time to solve classroom problems and develop curriculum materials. With a low ratio, the classroom should have a sense of order, and teachers will have more time to talk to parents. According to the Department of Early Education and Care for Infants and Preschool in Massachusetts, under the Standards for Licensure or Approval for Family Child Care, small group and school-aged child care programs have a required ratio for infants and toddlers (fifteen to thirty-three months) of one teacher for every four children. For preschoolers, the requirement is one teacher for every fifteen children (thirty-three months to kindergarten, or age five years). Our opinion is that preschoolers need two teachers in the classroom with fifteen children. All states have similar standards through departments of early education.

10. What type of accreditation does the preschool have? Are the teachers certified?

Preschools need to be accredited by the Department of Early Education and Care (DEEC), which is the state agency for Massachusetts. The DEEC requires one qualified preschool teacher certified by DEEC for every classroom. They may be accredited by the national agency, which is the National Association for Education of Young Children. Be sure that the teacher is certified and interacts well with children. It's important to find teachers who love their work with young children and show their enthusiasm as they talk to preschoolers. In Massachusetts there are regional offices under the DEEC that administer child care standards. There are many associations in many states that provide advocacy and help to parents who home-school their child. For example, in Massachusetts, there is the Massachusetts Homeschool Organization of Parent Educators (MassHOPE) and the Massachusetts Home Learning Association. Some parents may not be near a preschool and need to form their own at home. There are guidelines and associations to help with home school curriculum.

These questions identify the ideal preschool. There are also other questions to ask a preschool or a group of parents who may form a play group that may not have the specific resources to meet these ideal standards or may be a small parent cooperative at home.

11. How do your teachers accommodate different learning styles?

Some children may need a more structured classroom, while others may need a school that promotes more free play and less structure. If your child is shy and sensitive, she may need one-on-one encouragement to engage with peers. You will want to know if the preschool can accommodate this need.

12. What is the overall school philosophy?

It's important for you to feel that your child is in a school that promotes the same philosophy that you encourage in your family and your community. For example, the Friends School in Cambridge, Massachusetts, integrates a philosophy in school that encourages competence and confidence in analytical, critical, verbal, creative, mathematical, aesthetic, physical, and spiritual areas. The school's behavior guidelines are: Self-respect means—I am worthwhile; Respect for others means—You are worthwhile; Respect for property means—My school is worthwhile; Respect for safety means—We are all worthwhile.

Questions for Small Parent Cooperative Play Groups or Other Care Arrangements

Should I consider a cooperative preschool program?

Many parents decide to keep their child at home and extend their social and play time to include other children who are also at home. Sometimes these less formal preschool situations offer exceptional experiences. Parents arrange outings to playgrounds, farms, ponds, beaches, or museums that contribute to children's preschool education. They develop a core curriculum that includes many of the same topics that are covered in more formal preschools. They use the local library or the Internet to develop ideas for preschool activities. If this type of setting appeals to you, find a local cooperative play group that will allow your child to play at least for an hour each day.

What is the minimum adult-to-child standard in a preschool environment?

It is critical that there are enough adults to assist children who need any type of help. The minimum ratio for any preschool setting is the same as the ideal standards. The important point is for the parents to have some experience and not to put children together who are not a good fit or don't have similar needs and chemistry and can get along together during free play without major intervention.

THE STRATEGIES

The strategies outlined in the rest of the book are specifically developed to ensure that all children gets the most out of preschool experience so that they can be successful. This success can be quantified by their social and academic readiness for kindergarten. We have found that the most successful children share ten specific skills, or ways that they engage with other children. These skills are easy to identify and explain, and they can be taught. Mastering these skills in preschool can lead to specific and positive personality and temperament changes.

We've devised a program that defines a complex way of talking to children. These ideas and their implementation can be used with teachers in the preschool classroom as well as at home. We know that some skills, such as shyness, anxiety, and clumsiness, have a genetic component. Although preschool teachers and parents can help alleviate these tendencies or attributes in a child, these qualities may persist.

Each strategy is supported with illustrated cases of actual preschooler dialogues. From these you'll be able to glean how Ann works with preschoolers so that they learn the skills needed to develop and sustain friendships, increase their own social skills, and gain self-confidence in using language. What's more, you can use these same prompts in the dialogues with your own child. By using Ann's language, you can facilitate more focused conversation so that you can guide your child toward success with peers and help her develop these ten traits.

IN SUMMARY

- A child's developing brain is in a state of high plasticity during the preschool years, a critical time for learning.
- Children's success depends on the adults in their environment that will guide them toward the twelve skills to become compassionate, more confident, less anxious, and socially connected to peers.
- The best preschool situation, whether at home or in a formal environment, offers dramatic play because play and socialization are some of the most important paths to learning.

CHAPTER TWO

Raising a Likable Child

ALL PARENTS WANT THEIR CHILD to be likable. They want their child to feel good about himself, be able to say his name with confidence, enter any social group with ease, and connect to a community. At the same time, they hope that other children will want to play with their child. But are these goals realistic and achievable for every child? If your child is not naturally outgoing and confident, can these skills be taught? We believe that likability can not only be defined; it can be mastered.

This chapter will help you guide your child to be well liked by his peers, emotionally balanced, and able to cope with most situations around him. In our experience, a likable child is endearing, socially aware of others, shares, giggles and smiles, follows others' conversation, helps friends, understands what his friends are thinking, and knows how to laugh at problems in life. Most of all, a likable child is able to build long-term, meaningful friendships.

When a likable child is engaged, his face is vibrant, and his eyes sparkle. His smile, movements, facial expressions, and tone of voice all invite others to talk to him. He wants you to listen to him or to play. His hands stretch out toward others as they talk. His feet almost dance when he walks with peers. Some children who are likable are quiet and not talkative. These sensitive children smile, watch their peers, and use a gentle tone of voice, all of which causes others to be drawn to them.

All of these traits seem reasonable, but as we know, many children don't always behave in a likable manner. Or they are shy, uncomfortable around other children or adults, retreat in unfamiliar situations, or are off in their own world. If we can break down the characteristics of likability into functional categories, we can address them individually and then teach children to be more likable most of the time.

Likable children know how to

- Monitor their sensory needs
- Regulate their own emotions
- Understand another's perspective
- Recognize how to end play
- Take turns with peers
- Play with pretend power, not violence

CONNECTING LIKABILITY AND THE BRAIN

Our brain controls all aspects of our existence and every context of our lives, from the physical, to the emotional, to how we think about and perceive the world. During their earliest years, children begin to put all of these disparate pieces of development together. Some development seems to happen automatically, but the truth is that children are watching and learning as keen observers of the human behavior around them. They incorporate information from outside resources as they master bodily control, the structure of reason and thinking, and the different and subtle ways to recognize and manage their emotional state.

This development isn't finished by the time children are ready for preschool. In fact, between the ages of three and five, and sometimes even earlier, this period of change and brain plasticity is exactly when our most human traits and skills are beginning to develop and be refined. And more often than not, preschoolers need help from adults in order to become competent in the skills they need to interact, play, and develop friendships with other children. Just as they watched us model behavior when they were infants, they will continue to watch us model emotional and physical behavior for the next few years.

Understanding the World Through Sensory Integration

Sensory integration is the brain's ability to process information efficiently, and *praxis* is the process of translating an idea about an action into planning the action and executing that action.[1] When children's brains have too much or too little information, they become disorganized and can't respond in meaningful ways. Praxis involves the normal neurological progression of organizing fine and gross motor skills with postural and kinesthetic (awareness of body in space), ocular (control of eye movements and visual perception skills), and other sensory-motor abilities (planning for motor activities). These responses might include taking a hand away from a hot stovetop, organizing our bodies and space to walk down stairs, or coordinating our actions to climb up a slide.

Most preschoolers are just learning to fully integrate their senses into their lives. They cannot automatically make quick decisions in response to sensory stimulus. However, the most likable children do have the ability to integrate the external world into their own.

This is not easy. As we often describe to parents, a preschooler trying to master the stimulus of the outside world is like walking into a cocktail party that's already in full swing. No matter how much time you took to prepare yourself for a night out, when you walk in the door, you're instantly bombarded with the noise of other guests talking, music in the background, and people rushing over to greet you. Then someone hands you a drink and hors d'oeuvres before you've had a chance to survey the party. At first, you may retreat or pick out one person to talk to in order to enter a conversation. Meanwhile you're trying to balance your glass, your napkin, and maybe a purse. It will take some time before you feel comfortable enough to jump into the mix. This feeling of disorganization or unpredictability in a situation is similar to what preschoolers experience every day.

The likable child has mastered the art of simultaneously talking, playing, and moving with others. She can play with peers without over-reacting, or construct a story theme with toys and ignore the distracting sounds or bright lights. If one child accidentally bumps another, she might say, "Oops. Sorry. Didn't mean to crash into you!"

Being Sensitive or Shy

Not all children will have quite grasped all of this, and they may have difficulty adapting to the environment and to others. A child distracted by external stimuli will be unable to formulate his ideas in play, organize his thoughts, and, worse, won't be able to express those thoughts. Children who seem sensitive or shy may have difficulties with planning how close to move near a peer during play or how to monitor their voice in relation to their distance from a listener. One of the most complex tasks for any preschooler is to hold objects, run fast over bumpy playground areas, and talk to peers at the same time.

Here is an excellent example of children who have mastered sensory integration. In this case, Ann was teaching at a preschool in Boston, playing with four year olds as they were creating an imaginary rescue vehicle. The three boys were collecting sticks to create their rescue truck and running together in a tight pack. This activity required sensory integration skills to see the sticks, pick them up while moving, and run with their friends, all the while keeping their play going because they were following their plan of what they were going to do with the sticks next.

Their narrative developed because they were able to share ideas about how their "rescue operation" would take place while they continued to gather their pretend and real objects for their story theme. They monitored how close they were to each other and calculated where this rescue operation would begin. They screamed in delight as each child announced an idea for the story:

ALAN: I can put a rope from the truck to the mountain. (He points as he is running toward a hill in the sand area of the playground.)

CALEB: Yes! That's it. (Caleb races up the hill next to Alan and coordinates the position of the rope at the top.) This rope can go up the mountain. The kids are up there in the woods. They don't have any food.
JUSTIN: Oh, yes, we have to hurry! They are starving!

Alan is able to look at his peer, point, and run in order to direct the plan of the story. Caleb is able to respond to Alan while running and coordinate the rope placement. Justin runs near them, watching the activity of the rope and his friends, and talks while he runs.

The Many Facets of Sensory Integration

In 1979, A. Jean Ayres, renowned occupational therapist, was the first to recognize how senses are integrated, organized, and perceived for use by the brain for learning and function. She referred to this process of organizing sensory information for use as *sensory integration*. Sensory integration involves how we respond to and use a variety of inputs from our senses:

- The *tactile sense* provides information through our skin, such as how to detect the texture, shape, and size of objects in our environment.
- The *vestibular sense* through the inner ear provides a balance system and allows the body's smooth movement. It informs us about how our head and body position themselves within space through connections with our postural muscles and our eyes.
- The *proprioceptive sense*, delivered through our joints, muscles, and ligaments, sense and inform the brain of what our body is doing at any given time. It is important for allowing the child to have a good sense of his own body in space and is a primary mechanism for self-calming and organization of behavior. For example, proprioception allows a child to know how hard or soft to pet the family cat and how to maneuver around the desks and chairs in the classroom without running into things. For self-regulation, a child who

is overstimulated, such as at a birthday party, may seek proprioceptive information by crashing into other children or falling to the floor.[2]

Often any problems related to sensory integration are lumped together under a blanket diagnosis of "sensory integration issues," but there are many subcategories parents need to be aware of. One type of problem is called *dyspraxia*, which refers to difficulties with generating ideas for, planning, or executing motor actions. These problems originate with the child's difficulty in adequately processing and discriminating sensory inputs. Some preschoolers have trouble with planning, organizing, or carrying out a sequence of actions. Some educational neuropsychologists label this same dysfunction as "difficulty with executive function." In general terms, executive function means that a child has the ability to resist distraction, visual or auditory, and delay gratifications. It means that a child has *working memory*, which is the capacity to hold numbers or ideas in mind and think about them. The child also has *cognitive flexibility*, which is the presence of mind to adapt when demands change. Children spend most of their lives developing these skills as life becomes more complex. Preschoolers can learn these skills and acquire better executive function skills as they enter kindergarten.

Children who have problems coming up with ideas for motor skills may be rigid in their play and need others to lead in this area. Children with motor planning issues may have difficulty sequencing the small steps of a task, such as putting on a snowsuit or opening a backpack. In extreme cases, poor motor planning affects a child's ability to climb stairs, a process that requires putting one foot up and the other down to push up. They might struggle to keep upright, to balance, to time running and jumping. Often these children have problems completing common daily motor tasks such as getting dressed, eating, riding a bicycle, or cutting and coloring.

The child may find it hard to pour a liquid into a cup, climb onto a school bus, or organize the steps to make a sandwich. Some of these problems may not be obvious in children whose parents are willing to take the time to help them out. However, other children may find them frustrating to be around, and the child himself often realizes he is working harder than other children.

Some children have difficulty with self-regulation due to problems with *sensory modulation*. This problem is sometimes called a sensory modulation disorder. However, like dyspraxia, it is a specific type of sensory integration problem, not a separate issue. These children's understanding of the world is out of sync because their central nervous system can't regulate and respond correctly to sensory experiences. Consequently they often overreact to sensory messages that most other people do not find irritating or threatening. Overly reactive children may cover their ears or scream when they are exposed to loud noises, cry at the sound of a fire engine, or run away from children who are screaming or crying. They may withdraw or try to avoid bright lights, loud sounds, and noisy groups of other children. They may react with anger or irritation when touched or bumped unexpectedly and may dislike hugs and kisses. All of these responses, according to Carol Kranowitz, parent and author of *The Out-of-Sync Child Has Fun*, are "internal, unconscious, and invisible or out of the child's control."[3]

Children with sensory modulation problems may react to uncomfortable sensations by avoiding the inputs or seeking out calming and organizing inputs to counteract the noxious sensation. For instance, a child with touch sensitivity or tactile defensiveness may want to calm himself by craving the feeling of deep pressure: having his body pressed tightly against something else. Some hide under a beanbag chair in a classroom. Others may crash into their peers, seeking the tactile pressure that organizes them. This behavior can be misinterpreted by adults as being aggressive instead of a child's seeking sensory input.

Adults might easily mistake any of these behaviors characteristic of children with sensory integration problems and interpret their child as being willful, resistant, or belligerent. The truth is that these otherwise normal children are simply confused or overwhelmed by the bombardment of sensory input or the difficulty with managing what should be routine motor tasks. Children with sensory input issues are simply trying to organize themselves, control their movements, and integrate the sensory information that surrounds them. Therefore, children with these neurological and sensory issues need help in order for them to be able to function at their best.

Working on Sensory Integration at Home

Parents and teachers need to be both observant and hands on. Children need to develop self-regulation so they may react appropriately to the situation. Then they will be able to adjust to any situation without frightening, upsetting, or alienating other children. Children need help learning the intricacies of playing with objects smaller than they are, whether it is a doll, action figure, or another toy, and how they can use these in a story or a theme of play. They need direct support with handling the objects, as well as with the narrative they want to develop when they talk about their play.

At other times, adults need to be able to predict when the child requires alternative organizing sensory activities, such as swinging outside when the group is being too loud inside. Parents can create a sensory box, filled with small toys or crunchy food to help their child calm down. Crunchy pretzels and wind-up toys stimulate children in a tactile way. Many therapy toys are made just for sensory activities: squishy balls, blowing toys, sticks that move like an accordion and make noise, music boxes, small balls, and indoor trampolines.

If the child is not resistant to the presence of an adult, the adults should try to be close to the child during play, especially when he is playing with peers. They should use a soft voice and quietly coach the child with the language he can use to limit his peers so that they do not overwhelm him. You can suggest language cues like these:

- "I feel crowded."
- "You're too close."
- "Can I have more room?"

TIPS FOR SENSORY INTEGRATION AT HOME

- Set up a box of sensory items at home and at school.
- Provide a sensory corner at home or in the classroom.
- Give the child some language when he hesitates.
- Physically assist a child through a motor plan, such as opening a backpack or zipping up a snowsuit.
- Move slowly near the child and ask him if he is uncomfortable.
- Create a visual list or simple drawings of sensory activities that the child can use to choose. For example, create a language board that says, "I feel fidgety. I can choose!" Then list the various items that a child may need to calm himself. The list might include such things as chalk for drawing, a squishy ball to hold, pretzels to eat and crunch, shaving cream to squish on a table, wind-up toys that jump, and markers to draw on a white board.

Regulating Emotions

Along with the ability to regulate sensory input, children who can identify and control their emotions, and then adapt them to the emotions they see in other children, are better able to connect socially and become more likable. Children who can manage their emotions will not overreact or underreact to others. Once they learn to monitor their emotions and respond with some balance (not too overreactive or underreactive), they can develop better ways of relating and then become more likable.

Emotions are the adaptive psychological processes we experience, whether or not we recognize a particular trigger. Acquiring and mastering an emotional range takes time and practice because it is linked to all three areas of development: genetics, brain structure and function, and the plasticity of our changing brain.

The latest brain research shows that different parts of the brain, specifically the amygdala and the ventromedial prefrontal cortex, are associated with emotional regulation. Functional magnetic resonance imaging performed on adults shows that voluntary emotional regulation activates these regions in the brain.

Our emotional response is also connected to the release and production of hormones, including cortisol and oxytocin. Cortisol is usually referred to as the "stress hormone" because it is involved in response to stress and anxiety.

In a 2008 study from the University of Wisconsin, researchers H. Hill Goldsmith, S. D. Pollack, and R. J. Davidson showed that beyond brain chemistry or biology, there is a specific interconnection of skills involved with modulating emotional responses. These researchers believe that emotional processes in children don't develop automatically, but instead require both biological development and complex learning. In their words, "These affective processes become increasingly intricate as relevant neuroanatomical and neurophysiologically systems mature, suggesting that more sophisticated emotional skills might rely solely on the growth of relevant neural substrates."[4]

The emotional experiences of children are likely to organize their affective neural circuitry. The findings suggest that caregivers who provide positive emotional experiences create long-term effects for later behavior. Other studies confirm these findings. For example, studies conducted on abused, neglected, or isolated children routinely show that they experience delays in learning to differentiate the facial expressions of emotion. In such instances, the environment, more than genetics or brain structure, may have a bearing on children's ability to connect with others.

Research related to the connections between the brain and the link to emotions, however, is still unclear. Dr. Jerome Kagan, professor of psychology at Harvard and author of *The Long Shadow of Temperament*, has studied children for decades and believes that "no FMRI can generate a brain profile that will allow an investigator to predict with confidence whether a person is, at that moment, feeling happy, sad, proud, or guilty."[5]

Special Children

Some studies have sought to better define these connections by viewing a child's emotions through studies of abused, neglected, or isolated children. This research has shown that these children experience delays in learning to differentiate the facial expressions of emotion. If these children are limited in reading the subtle language cues of others, such as facial expression, they may have difficulty relating to peers during play interactions. In such instances, the environment, along with the child's genetics or brain structure, may have an impact on the child's ability to connect with others.

We agree with many of these studies based on our own experience of working with autistic children. We're currently able to identify areas where emotional regulation needs to be addressed, and when we do, the child can learn to modify his behavior. However, we can't assume that particular interventions during this time of immense brain plasticity can lead to permanent neural changes and foster recovery. Yet we can say that many children who are treated intensively and early during these preschool years make significant progress and become more emotionally adjusted.

Emotional development is rapid during the first five years of life. Studies have shown that year-old children already understand anger, sadness, enjoyment, fear, interest, and surprise. Within the second year of life, guilt, shame, embarrassment, and pride emerge. Toddlers can connect their emotions with a situational context: they know what makes them happy and can replicate that happiness.

Between the ages of three and five, children learn to regulate their emotions in order to form friendships and express how they feel. Four year olds are beginning to notice other children's emotions and respond to them with the same emotion. They don't overreact. Instead, they make connections by adapting to their peer's emotional state. Preschoolers who easily grasp the concept of regulating their own emotions become likable.

Many preschool children are more than emotionally sensitive: they lack the skills to deal with the strong emotions of others and often respond with their own frustration and anger, combined with aggressive behavior. Sensitive and shy children may retreat behind a table or refuse to use language to express their feelings when they face unfamiliar situations. Kagan, who has studied temperament in children for decades, reported that "having a temperamental bias does not mean that adolescents or adults are not responsible for their behavior. People with healthy brains are able to control their actions, even though they may be less able to impose equivalent control over their feelings."[6]

Kagan writes that although the concept of temperament, or having an "emotional tone," implies an inherited physiology that is linked to emotions and behaviors, the nature of this link is poorly understood. Some children freeze in place if an adult comes into a room with a mask or flee if a large dog runs toward them, but some remain immobile for a long time and will cry for hours after they flee from the dog. Dr. Kagan believes that "on the basis of research . . . inherited temperamental biases, combined with life experiences, create this variation in behavior reaction to unfamiliar events."[7] This means that we need to help children who may be more sensitive to unfamiliar situations than others through our engagement with them in play experiences.

We believe that many children are vulnerable to the stress and conflict that often accompany play and peer interactions. Over the past thirty years, we have been working with children with language disabilities and have found that some children may throw things, stomp their feet, push their body into others, and show their emotions with overt gestures. If these children have some temperamental bias toward reactions to the unfamiliar, as Kagan explains in his book, it is essential that teachers and parents assist these children through planned intervention that will help them recover from their emotional reaction to new situations in order to make peer connections.

If some children are quickly redirected or guided with appropriate support, they can avoid the cycle, and the tantrums will diminish. Other children may need the support of a teacher or a parent who uses specific strategies directed at helping children engage in social situations. That's why it is so important for parents and teachers to understand emotional regulation, sensitive and shy children, as well as children with sensory integration needs so that they can help preschoolers during play.

Working with Children to Foster Emotional Development

You can point out other children's emotions during play by helping your child identify the facial expressions and body language that are the clues to interpreting an emotional reaction. Sometimes when preschoolers get excited, adults instinctively want to calm them down. Without realizing that this can be an opportunity to point out a child's emotions, the adult may ignore the overreaction and ask the child to be quiet. We believe that the adult ought to point out a child's reaction to by saying, "Oh, wow, you must be so excited! You look so happy! I bet you can't wait to . . . !"

It is also important to allow time for children to recognize each other's emotions. Preschoolers run fast and are interested in toys and the world around them. Sometimes they miss the subtle or overt cues of body language, facial expression, and volume that help us see how another person might be feeling.

As they learn to recognize the emotions in others, they will want to make connections and join in with other children to play. But even when a preschooler moves from parallel play to joined play, she still might need a parent's or a teacher's support. One skill to work on is called *joint attention*, which means two or more children sharing a single event. A child who enters into joint attention immediately moves near the other child, shows him a toy, or gestures and points to something that both can see is happening. They will engage in back-and-forth exchange of body language, facial expressions, and comments to each other, showing that they are sharing not only a toy but an event.

In order to complete this skill, both children need to know how to regulate their emotions. When a child enters a setting and wants to make a connection with a peer, she must be able to monitor her emotions as she shares and talks with the child. If she is sharing an event, she must be responding with the right emotions, facial expression, and body language. When children experience joint attention, they have the opportunity to verbalize their emotions. According to Rebecca Landa, who studies peer interactions, joint attention is the crucial and pivotal skill in social communication and a precursor to the development of a child's ability to see the perspective of others.[8] As children share, watch, and listen to each other, they feel connected, and they like each other. They know their friends feel what they feel.

The Help That Adults Can Give

The following dialogue shows how an adult can guide the recognition of emotional reactions. Ann was working on the social skills of Erin and Marley, two four-year-old girls who had never before met each other. Both girls were social in some respects because they wanted to be with other children, but they didn't know what to say or how to act when they were with friends.

The girls came to Ann's office and stood with their mothers just outside the door. When Ann opened the door, both were looking down at their feet. Ann knelt near the girls to be at their eye level and motioned for them to look at each other.

Erin looked as if she was about to cry, and Marley just stared down at the floor. Ann prompted Erin to turn her shoulder toward Marley and say, "Hi, I'm Erin. I'm shy."

Marley immediately shouted, "I'm too loud! My mommy says that I don't talk, I scream!" Erin covered her ears with her hands and shut her eyes tight.

ANN: Marley, do you think that Erin is afraid when you talk loud?

MARLEY: (Stood tall and shook her head to say no.)

ANN: How do you feel Erin?

ERIN: Scared. (She whispered and turned her body away from Marley. Marley looked at Ann.)

ANN: Marley, what is Erin doing?

MARLEY: She's looking away.

ANN: Okay, what do you think that means? Is Marley happy?

MARLEY: (in a screaming voice again) No, she's NOT happy!

Ann led them into the playroom where they both ran for a small box of wind-up toys. Erin turned the knob of the robot, and it started to make noise and walk. Marley giggled. Marley turned the knob of the butterfly that ran across the table and fell to the floor. Erin giggled. Ann picked up the toys.

ANN: How are you now?

ERIN: (smiled and whispered) I'm silly!

MARLEY: (in a softer voice) She's happy!

ANN: Marley, how did Erin feel when you used such a loud shouting voice? (Marley smiled and giggled and didn't answer.)

ERIN: (in a louder voice) I was afraid! (Marley laughed and looked at Erin. They both giggled and turned the knobs of two small music boxes.)

ANN: Do you like music? (They both nodded their heads and jumped up, waving their music boxes.) Are you feeling happy or sad or afraid now?

ERIN: (now in a shouting voice with a laugh) I am not afraid! I love music.

Marley moved closer to Erin, leaned her body in toward her, and touched her shoulder as she handed her the butterfly.

Ann was able to get the girls to acknowledge their own emotions and the emotions of each other. She accomplished this by pointing out the subtle cues that allow children to see the emotions of others. A child who turns away might be scared or afraid. A child who is jumping with glee and waving a toy is probably happy.

Your goal is to suggest language that is age appropriate for your child so that she can express emotions. You will need to be creative and use language that fits the conversation. If a child doesn't imitate or use your suggestions, she may not be ready to say it or may not be thinking this way. If she does use the language exactly or vary it, she is probably thinking and feeling they way you thought.

THE COMMON TEMPERAMENTS OF LIKABLE CHILDREN

Likability can also be measured in terms of social maturity and temperament. Even at young ages, children are beginning to understand the ways people differ and how they think. According to Alison Gopnik, author of *The Philosophical Baby*, "From two to six, children discover fundamental facts about how their own minds and the minds of others work."[9] They see that people differ in their beliefs, perceptions, emotions, and desires and that these differences lead to different actions.

In this way, children can make inferences about what others are experiencing. In one experiment, Gopnik showed a group of four-year-old children a toy bunny in a basket. The children were told that the bunny was scared of some animals but not others. They showed the children a zebra, and the bunny shook with fear. But when they showed the children an elephant, the bunny welcomed him. Next, the elephant and the zebra both showed up in the basket. The bunny shook with fright. The four year olds drew the right conclusions about what made the bunny scared. They perceived that the zebra frightened the bunny, so even before they were asked to, they removed it from the basket to give the bunny peace of mind. The following are some distinct characteristics of social maturity that likable children usually attain.

Likable Children Understand the Perspective of Others

If we point out the emotions of others, we are helping them recognize how their peers' actions may differ. Gopnik says, "Children who can explain actions in terms of theory of mind also seem more adept, for good or ill, at altering other people's minds. Children who better understand minds are more socially skillful than those who do not."[10]

A likable child can acknowledge a friend who is happy, angry, sad, or disappointed and can respond to these emotions in kind. Your goal is to create experiences during play with peers that help the child express thoughts and feelings and perceive others' emotions.

One of our favorite anecdotes occurred at the farm preschool where Ann works. She was walking with a group of preschoolers toward a duck pond. One big duck had a distinct white pom-pom on top of her head. As the group got closer to the ducks, we could see them all flapping and squawking at each other, running back and forth in the water. It was early spring, and some ice patches were still floating in the pond.

One child yelled out, "Look, Ann! They are fighting!"

Ann knew right away that the ducks looked as if they were fighting, but in fact they were mating. The teacher turned toward Ann, her hand over her mouth. She whispered, "Oh, no, I'm not ready to explain the facts of life to these kids!"

As we approached the ducks, the children tried to feed them grain, but the ducks were not interested.

TIBBIN: They aren't hungry. What are they thinking?

JAYDA: They are so mad. They are having a big fight. Look they want to be near the duck with the pom-pom.

ANN: Well, they might be fighting over who gets to be close to who. Right?

TIBBIN: (with hands on his hips, yelled at the duck who was doing the most squawking) You stop this yelling! You can't have this duck! Be nice to her!

ANN: Okay, let's decide who is a happy duck and who might be angry.

JOSIE: He's very angry.

ANN: Okay, so what is he thinking about?

JAYDA: He wants to be near that duck! See?

ANN: Do you think that ducks think?

ALL THE CHILDREN: Yes! Yes.

ANN: Do some ducks think different things than other ducks do?

DANIEL: Well, that duck over there is under the bush, and he is think-ing, "I want some grain!"

JAYDA: Yeah, that duck is thinking that she is afraid. I don't want to be a duck. They fight too much. I'd be afraid.

Ann was using the ducks as a metaphor for a child experiencing others' emotions. When children see changes in animals, they connect these changes and emotions to their own feelings. Ann asked questions to help them think about what someone else might be thinking. The fact that ducks may think differently helps them understand that we all have different ideas. This is the first step in learning to see the per-spectives of others. In peer relationships, children need to understand more complex emotions and ideas that will come from their friends. But at the duck pond, they can begin to identify concrete emotions such as happiness, sadness, and anger by observing the animals' behav-iors in a natural setting.

Likable Children Recognize How to End Play

During the preschool years, children often leave another child out by walking away or moving toward another peer, ignoring the first child. The child who is left becomes angry and disappointed. He may think that the child who left him is angry at him and therefore he shouldn't express his anger or the other child might get even angrier. Children at this age (and frankly, people at any age) need to feel comfortable enough to express anger at friends and realize that this expression of anger is part of being in a relationship. The key to success is how to express angry feelings or other emotions and how to interpret these feelings and ideas in others. Children also need to know that friends can be angry at each other and remain friends.

Likable Children Learn from Adults About Expressing Feelings

You can intervene in a play situation when two or three children are angry by naming the emotions each child is feeling and supporting the child when he expresses his anger toward his friends. One technique is to find a new shared interest that will bring the two children together. For example, if two children are fighting over a toy, you can help them construct a new play scenario that will make them both happy.

Here is an example of one child feeling left out and the other child not realizing that he rejected his peer. In this dialogue, Ann is playing with Jerry and Carter and their small toy planes. Suddenly Carter flies his plane away and leaves Jerry alone.

JERRY: I want him to come back.

ANN: You want him to come back. You feel mad.

JERRY: Yeah. (nods head and pouts)

ANN: Why do you feel mad?

JERRY: Because he went away.

ANN: Can you . . . Jerry, tell Carter you want him to come back? Carter, are you gonna go back and play? (Carter moves closer to Jerry and starts to move a car and make loud car noises, not looking up at Jerry.) So, Carter, can you tell Jerry you're back to play now?

CARTER: I'm back to play!

JERRY: Yep.

ANN: So, Carter, when you run off without telling him, he feels sad. You can run away and change what you are doing, but you have to say, "I'm going over here! I'm going to play over here," if you change. Right?

Jerry is able to state how he feels, but he didn't have the tools to get Carter back to his play. Ann was able to validate his feelings by giving him the opportunity to explain his feelings. When Carter hears Jerry's feelings, he returns to play.

Children need experience in listening to how a friend feels about their relationship. In this case, Carter needed to hear how Jerry was missing him and how he really liked him and wanted him to play. When Ann helped Carter return to listen to Jerry's feelings, she helped both boys. They learned that friends can feel disappointed and still remain friends and continue playing. Jerry learned that if you tell your friend that you miss him, your friend learns that you really like him. Carter learned how to make a switch in play without hurting his friend's feelings. Once he responds this way, he'll be seen as kinder and more likable to his friends.

Likable Children Take Turns

Children want to "own" the toys they are using and play in parallel, often talking about their own actions. Some three year olds scream for a toy if another child enters their play area, especially if that child grabs the toy. It is common for a three year old to march up to another three year old and grab a doll. We all know what happens next: one of the two children will be crying, screaming, pulling, yanking, or hitting.

Often a parent's first response to this situation is to make the children share. The parent might talk to the child who has taken the toy or address the child who originally had the toy. The parent might say to the one who is holding the doll, "Tell her she can have the doll in one minute."

If you have tried this before, you know that this line of reasoning usually doesn't work with three years olds. It is also typical for a parent to say this to the child while standing up or talking from another room.

Instead, you need to get down to the child's level and provide enough language for both girls to help the situation. An example of how one mother resolved a conflict between two sisters fighting over a doll follows. One child was smacking the other with the doll and running in the opposite direction from the other. Both were screaming. The mother stayed by them, followed one girl and then the other as they screamed. When there was a moment of silence between the girl's screams, she responded with her body language and facial expression that showed how concerned she was about their despair. She knelt down on one knee to be at their level and started this conversation:

MOM: Gail, you need to say, "May I have a turn, please?"

GAIL: May I have a turn, please?

MOM: (turns to Cathy) Cathy, Gail's gonna have a turn for one minute. Then you say, "May I have a turn, Gail?" Then you'll get a turn! You have to wait for one minute. (Mom praises Gail for waiting. Cathy gives the doll to Gail.) Thank you. (Gail suddenly gives the doll to Cathy.) Thank you, Gail! (She shows her own affect [emotional response in her kind voice tone and in her facial expression] as she praises Gail.) That was so nice of you! That was so nice. (Mom pats Gail on the cheek and gives her a kiss.) Thank you. (Gail smiles.) Look how happy Cathy is with the doll. Thank you, Gail.

By pointing out Cathy's emotional reaction, Gail realized that Cathy was going to give her a turn and that she did understand her feelings of losing this doll. When Gail waits, her mother praises her for waiting and giving Cathy the time to be with the wanted doll. The mother is teaching her child not only patience but how to become sensitive to the feelings of others. Gail can repeat this skill in another situation, and she will become more likable to her friends. They will want to play with her, and they will include her in play.

Likable Children Play with Limited Power, Not Violence

Children today play with the violent themes they are exposed to in the media and in real life. It is a normal part of a child's emotional development to want to have some sense of power or control. However, many preschoolers today see far too many violent themes on television, in movies, on the computer on YouTube, and even on their parents' iPhone.

While preschoolers often play out themes they've seen on television, their play may also reflect the way they are feeling at any given moment. Or play themes might be attributed to a child's personality. A child who is a risk taker may crave lots of sensation during play. More sensitive children who might be temperamentally inhibited may choose themes that involve fear.

Current research on play and violence suggests that the teacher or the parent must expand the child's play by introducing new themes, including themes on warmth, love, or healing, such as a vet taking care of a sick puppy. Stanley Greenspan, a child psychiatrist who is famous for his work in the field of children with autism, suggests that you can help children build empathy if you become an emotional part of their play themes.[11] For example, in Ann's technique of Narrative Play therapy, she suggests that parents and teachers become a peer during play in order to suggest creative ways to extend play themes into new character roles that incorporate less violent actions.

Jane Katch makes the point in her book, *Under Deadman's Skin: Discovering the Meaning of Children's Violent Play*, that children need balance within their play. They need to be exposed to some violent themes with clear restrictions (no blood, chopping people up, or killing, and no laughing at this action), and at the same time they need to be in constant dialogue with their teachers and parents about how they feel when they are confronted with these aggressive play themes. Katch found that children were able to follow as well as set reasonable rules as well as limits on violent play, including length of play and play themes.[12] Perhaps she has found the answer in this controversial area of children's play.

We believe that everyone involved in the play theme needs to agree to the play guidelines. For example, if a child is going to be hurt or is simply afraid of violent play, the teacher or parent needs to set a rule for their play, such as, "no swinging light sabers at each other." The key is to engage in active dialogue before the play begins, as well as monitor what children are exposed to in the media.

The way digital images morph into scary monsters and the way videographers cut and move clips so quickly creates a fast-moving, overwhelming visual story that often scares children (and even adults). News programs that used to feature a reporter sitting at a desk have changed to a more stimulating and graphic approach, with loud sounds and film clips that move faster than a race car. A child can be eating cereal for breakfast and viewing the Iraq War and see bloodshed in high definition. Children today want to imitate this fast pace and often the violence and power in these films in order for them to try to understand what is going on.

Some children are more physical and want more power during their play, yet there are limitations that will make even violent play more socially acceptable. When children actually scare other children, that's when the violent play should be redirected. For instance, a child should never put his hands in another child's face: children are often scared of that action of another person in close proximity. Some play themes are not acceptable, like killing others with knives, or chopping others into pieces, or shoving high-kicks in a child's face or shooting. These themes make the child appear less likable, and the rest of the children may respond with unease and retreat.

By changing the theme during play, you can give your child other options to create pretend personas with power but without the violence. For example, a shark is powerful because it has to be in order to survive. Pretending to be a powerful shark is more socially acceptable than running around shooting people.

Ann was once watching two preschoolers, Marc and Jordan, who were playing cops and robbers with police boats. The boys' story included having the cops chop off the heads of the robbers, or drown them, or refuse to give the robbers any food and water. Ann tried to redirect them, giving the police a more humanitarian mission. She created a story line where the police boat goes to other countries with children to bring them food. The boys picked up on that theme and continued to play. They became calm and less interested in chopping off the robbers' heads.

Preschool teacher Janet Craig told Ann, "When I first came here, everybody was obsessed with *Star Wars*, and they would fight. They would throw each other on the ground, and it was getting out of hand.

So we bought Star Wars Legos and let them channel the same feeling into building."[13]

On the other side, children need the right language to excuse themselves from the violent play of others. Teachers and parents need to listen to them if they are afraid and set a strong limit on how they play in order to be inclusive. Teaching them to use language can be as easy as saying, "I don't want to play that game," or "I don't think that is a good thing." And "Stop. I'm not comfortable playing that," sends a clear message to the child who wants to use violent themes that his ideas won't go over and his friends may retreat.

TIPS FOR ENCOURAGING EMOTIONAL BALANCE

The following techniques will help ensure that your child gets closer to the core characteristics of a likable child.

Talk with Your Child About Violent Themes, and Limit Exposure to the Media

Plenty of television shows and computer games geared to young children contain violent themes, even if they are presented with cartoon characters and bright colors. Study after study has linked viewing violence with incorporating it into play. Although it is very difficult to ban television and computer games altogether, you can work with your child to set distinct time limits that he is comfortable with. This way, he feels that he is in control, and you are able to limit the content of his own violent themes.

Talk About a Child's Actions and Ideas Instead of Drilling a Child with Questions

This nonconfrontational conversation style creates an environment that leads to children wanting to be together and in a cohesive group. A child who is confronted with constant questioning from a parent or teacher may shut down or stop responding. A question might feel like a test where the child needs to "perform." Instead, when you enter a situation with your child, simply notice what is going on and then talk about the actions. This will help you become a part of the group, and you will be less threatening to your child and the other children.

Praise Your Child for Acknowledging Someone Else's Situation and Helping Others

These traits are the building blocks that encourage empathy. Use praise constantly for even small, concrete behaviors. You will be signaling to your child that you are validating his brave attempt to help others. He will then seek out other opportunities and not ignore situations when others need help.

Model Correct, Genuine Emotional Responses. Use Language That Expresses Your Feelings

Your child watches everything you do. Eventually she is able to copy not only your language but your affect. Your relationship with your child is the most important part of helping her see real emotions. This positive modeling will help her trust her own emotions when she sees how she feels and when her response matches yours. Best of all, you will become one of her peers because she will understand that she can relate to you.

Create Schedules Whenever Possible, and Prepare Your Child for Transitions

This will help support the child who is temperamentally inhibited to unfamiliar situations, including new sounds and places. Use a calm, soft voice to explain the transition and what might occur. Then when you arrive at the unfamiliar situation, whether it is a new classroom, playground, or even a play date, continue to use a soft voice and direct your conversations away from your own child and toward her peers. This will show your child that you are accepting the new children and the new situation, and she will then model your behavior. If this strategy is not working, give your child time to retreat with you so that she can regroup and then reenter the scene. Stay for a few moments, and praise your child for making eye contact, or turning toward a peer, or engaging in conversation. Soon you will find that you will be working with your child with one peer, and then two to three.

Once children learn to regulate their emotions, and play with peers with story themes that they create together, they will build new friendships immediately. The next step is to make sure that they are self-confident and happy with themselves as they form these new friendships.

IN SUMMARY

- Likable children can monitor their emotions and tell teachers or parents when they need a break.
- Likable children will learn to see the perspective of others and consider others' needs when they interact and play.
- Children are naturally drawn to those who possess the quality of self-awareness, can regulate their emotions, and are confident.

CHAPTER THREE

Preparing an Achieving Child

LIKE MANY OTHER PARENTS of preschoolers, you might already be concerned about your child's academic future. It's not unusual for parents to begin to worry about the demands that will be placed on their child's performance after preschool. Parents may be concerned about early success because some believe it can have a major impact on future accomplishment, ranking, and placement in higher educational settings. So for many parents, a lot is at stake here.

This chapter is meant to ease the anxiety that parents and teacher face as they try to meet the demands of this generation of educational constraints, testing, and academic achievement. The latest research states that play during the preschool years is firmly connected to academic achievement by the elementary school years: children do not necessarily need direct teaching or a reduction of play in their preschool day in order to succeed.

Some of this anxiety is coming directly from schools. Teachers are under pressure from their administrators to prepare preschoolers for the rigors of the academic load they face in elementary school. Teachers are also responding to parents who want their child to achieve academically, which is often measured by having the ability to read early and understand basic math.

Both teachers and parents are also concerned about federal mandates designed to keep our national test scores as high as in other countries. In Boston, where we work, for example, parents of preschoolers already know about the ways that public schools are funded and are concerned about getting their child ready to take specific standardized tests that will dictate whether their schools will receive additional funding from the state. At the same time, their pride is on the line for their child to excel on these tests. So it's no wonder that many parents believe that their youngest children will face challenges that seem to be greater than any child faced even as recently as five years ago.

WHAT'S REALLY GOING ON AT PRESCHOOL TODAY

These real and perceived issues have changed the face of the preschool day. The emphasis in some preschools has changed to meet these concerns of parents, and programs are becoming more academically oriented.

The Decline of Socialization

What used to be two or three hours of socialization is now becoming half- or full-day programs where the goal of academic success has overridden the longer-standing tradition of developing social skills.

Many schools are eliminating recess time in favor of making more time for academics. Some preschools are using worksheets to go over premath and prereading, and they are extending circle time in order to cover the direct teaching of academic skills. For example, a preschool teacher may gather the class in circle time and review the day's schedule. Then the group will be required to sit quietly and listen to a lesson about phonics or about particular academic subjects such as math and science.

One parent told us, "My preschooler is expected to be reading! He is told to read and write short stories as well as draw pictures in preschool."

Yet preschoolers can get fidgety and inattentive. Many of them don't have the capacity to sit and listen. Instead they want to be engaged in a more active way. Worse, while they are sitting and fidgeting, they are suffering the consequences of not playing. David Elkind, professor emeritus in the Eliot-Pearson Department of Child Development at Tufts University, notes in his 2007 book, *The Power of Play*, that these changes in the structure and content of preschools are contributing to the suppression of children's curiosity, imagination, and fantasy.[1]

While many parents and teachers believe that direct teaching is the correct route to academic prowess, current and past research has shown that peer connections through social engagement during a free play setting can be quantified as one of the best methods for achieving success in elementary school, with results lasting as long as the third grade.

Countless studies have shown that worksheets, formal lessons, and other methods of direct teaching are not necessarily the best path to academic achievement. Instead, researchers have proven over and over again that young children need outside time, free play, and unstructured social activities during their day in order to learn academic skills.

The Value of Free Play

A 1999 study from the National Association for the Education of Young Children found that preschoolers can acquire complex mathematical concepts and applications when learning material incorporated into free play. Similar studies of early academic skills found that when literacy and reading is incorporated into imaginative play with some adult help, children learn faster than if they are taught directly at a desk or in circle time. In one 2002 study of low-income preschool children, researchers found that "those who play competently with their peers are more actively engaged in classroom learning activities and conversely, children who are lacking in play skills are inattentive, passive, and lack motivation."[2]

In one Yale study on play, researchers Dorothy G. Singer, Jerome Singer, Sharon Plaskon, and Amanda Schweder found that "play has been shown to foster an impressive array of skills that are necessary for school success."[3] Imaginative play is directly linked to these skills, among others:

- Understanding another child's perspective, which leads to seeing a shared interest with others and the ability to solve academic problems in a cooperative group
- Regulating one's emotions, which leads to maintaining an even temperament in school so that the child can focus on academic concepts instead of social distractions
- Taking turns with classmates, which leads to negotiation skills that link directly to learning
- Sequencing the order of events, which leads to abstract reasoning skills
- Recognizing one's independence from others, which leads to the ability to complete an academic task

Free play and recess time give children important access to practice relating to peers, retelling their ideas, and applying logical reasoning, all necessary components for later academic success. At the same time, they are learning to make emotional adjustments to situations with other children and finding shared interests, which leads to creating a sense of community.

Yet despite all of this important research, the U.S. Department of Education's *Guide to U.S. Department of Education Programs 2009*, which lists the outcomes deemed desirable for children in high-quality preschool programs, does not include social skills.[4] This is why it is so important for teachers and parents to take responsibility for creating not just free but supervised social connections in a facilitated play setting that helps children to advance and achieve academic success.

THE BEST EXPERIENCE: FACILITATED PLAY

Not all free play opportunities are created equal. Sometimes teachers stand back and observe preschoolers during free play instead of engaging with them. They may believe that they are watching children interact with others if they are playing near peers and having conversations.

In reality, these young preschoolers are in parallel play. They may be next to each other, but they are nevertheless playing alone. At home, parents often observe their children playing with others at the local park playground and assume that they are engaged. They watch them follow other children going up a slide and feel that they are having fun. However, unless the parent is actively engaged in the experience, the child is getting only half the benefits. Without adult input during play, children are not getting the help they need to advance, because they don't have the skills to engage in negotiation or develop complex ideas with other children. The truth is that preschoolers need help with social engagement with other preschoolers.

This help is referred to as *language facilitation*. During play, adults can help a child notice what a peer is doing, or help create a story about their play. Parents can monitor that their child is not only playing near peers but playing with them: interacting and sustaining a real conversation.

HOW THE BRAIN RESPONDS TO FACILITATED FREE PLAY

Many neuroscientists believe that in the first years of a child's life, tens of thousands of synaptic connections are made each second in the brain, opening the door for increased learning capacity. This creates a window of opportunity for learning, especially for children to under-stand language at a higher level.

There is no technology yet to verify these ideas. But our work with autistic children has shown us that intensive early intervention that is specifically conducted during facilitated free play can result in considerable changes in behavior, which signify, and in our minds quantify, brain growth and enhanced development. For example, as we watch our patients during play therapy, we can see positive changes take place in their abilities. Not every child is a complete success story, but most of our patients don't regress to their former behavior patterns; they move forward and change to become more in the mainstream.

Neuroscience backs up our findings. When we engage in social interactions, we know that specific patterns of activity are taking place in our brains that do not occur when we are alone. Brain activity gets imprinted over time, much as we experience muscle memory in our arms and legs. And like all other muscles in the body, the brain has a use-it-or-lose-it capacity. If we don't activate the brain in every possible way, it won't reach its full potential.

Furthermore, although it is believed that these brain changes may occur throughout life, research has suggested that brain changes are more likely and more easily obtained in the very young brain, which is considered to be more plastic than the older, adult brain, which is often referred to as "hard wired." The effects of intensive early inter-vention and therapies support this contention.

Animal studies have begun to provide evidence for changes that occur in the brain as the result of intervention. For example, rodents provided with a physically stimulating environment will develop many more dendrites (nerve fibers), protoplasmic extensions (a colorless material comprising the living part of a cell including the nucleus) of their nerve cells, than other rodents that have been allowed to be more sedentary. Thus, at least physical intervention in the animal appears to improve the development and structure of nerve cells and their con-nections to each other. It seems likely that other types of interventions may play a similar role with similar outcomes, although we have little research so far to securely support this hypothesis.

These behavioral and developmental changes may reflect positive advances in the neurobiology of the human brain, but we really don't know yet exactly how this relates to connectivity, neurochemical changes, more neurons, fewer neurons, or what else. But there's another new scientific area of research, theory, and application.

Current research in face processing, which is the ability to understand and interpret the faces of those around us, has been a topic of considerable interest for neuroscientists. Much of the research has implicated the fusiform gyrus of the brain and its connections with the amygdala, a brain structure believed to be important for decoding emotion and behavior. Data from studies in young children have supported the role of experience in brain specialization, with the parts of the brain known to be involved in face processing beginning to come on line during the first year of life.[5] Visual exposure and social environment are both believed to play a critical role, and that experience is crucial for the development of many perceptual and cognitive functions, and probably emotional and social interaction as well, has been documented. This research will begin to open up avenues for further study of social relatedness and how these skills develop in young children.

Until then, we can say only that it is clear that change can happen during this unique window of opportunity during the preschool years, and it seems that the most advanced children are taking advantage of this unique place in time.

HOW TO FACILITATE FREE PLAY

All play doesn't happen naturally. Children need to learn to engage in play that is productive and a happy event for everyone involved. This means that children benefit when an adult, whether a teacher or a parent, assists during play interactions. Sue Brendekamp, director of research at the Council on Professional Recognition in Washington, D.C., reports that if a teacher is frequently involved in "free play" as a coplayer in supporting children's play by guiding, modeling, demonstrating, and elaborating on language in one-to-one conversations, children will not get stuck in immature, repetitive play. This is crucial for developing vocabulary, language skills, and interactions with other children. Children who are engaged in sociodramatic free play are better able to see the perspective of others. Research has found consistent links between free play during preschool and long-term language growth in the classrooms. Preschoolers with these skills will be better prepared for school and achieve greater academic success in the elementary school years with a higher vocabulary and more social competence.[6] David Dickinson, chair and professor, Department of Teaching and Learning, Vanderbilt University's Peabody's College, found "consistent links between kindergarten measures and the total number of words and variety of words that children used during free play when they were in preschool as four year olds. The most effective teachers were those who were selective in choice of words, using relatively sophisticated words, and were reciprocal in conversation."[7]

Adults can take on many roles during facilitated play: observer, stage manager, or coplayer. Brendekamp believes that the observer determines when to intervene, the stage manager provides play themes and organizes the sequence of play, and the coplayer involves himself or herself in the play, scaffolds language, and helps the children extend the play.

At the same time, the adult has to be careful not to take over the child's play or the child may resist. Parents and teachers need to be discrete, becoming one of the peers, and join their children in play so the instruction is subtle. You will be suggesting language or themes, helping them make the connections themselves. Then as the children begin to connect, you'll need to fade back and let them learn from each other.

Try to incorporate facilitated play during each day. In this way, your child will achieve a higher set of complex language skills, along with the ability to understand abstract concepts and organize their thoughts into a logical sequence. Each of these goals will contribute to later academic achievement, as well as emotional adjustment, independence, and self-confidence.

Let's look at some strategies for this kind of facilitated play.

Bring the Outdoors to Life

The goal of this strategy is to use the environment as one of many characters in dramatic facilitated play. Children love the outdoors, and their environment is a place that can be a helpful "character" to an adult who is trying to get children to engage socially and learn new vocabulary. The "character" can be a falling leaf on a pond, or a duck quacking, or a pony in the pasture eating grass, or a mound of dirt that they can climb. Preschoolers love to be muddy, run along a fence, and talk to each other as they engage in sharing the environment.

Emotionally adjusted children play and engage with friends as well as with the environment. Everything around them becomes part of their engagement with each other. If a parent encourages the child to observe, listen, and talk about the environment with others, the child will be captivated by the experience and want to share it with another person. She will engage in joining others.

Act as a keen observer of nature and narrate a story using any one of the many aspects of your environment. You are providing creative experiences, increasing the use of meaningful words, building your child a rich vocabulary at a high language level, and promoting logical reasoning and organizational skills as well as socialization.

You can bring a child to a farm and teach her new vocabulary words, associate actions of animals with new abstract concepts such as the seasons, or even teach a child the qualities that make a good friend. When children have the ability to talk about the leaves or animals or what is nearby at a park playground, they can draw other children into their conversation, encouraging children to talk to each other. They will make comments as they watch what is happening around them.

When children are excited about their surroundings and connect with others, they are happy and others are drawn to them.

Some parents are reticent to bring groups of children to natural settings because they feel that they will lose control of them. Or parents will take children to a natural setting with a specific task in mind, like apple picking or petting animals. Sometimes the adult tries to direct the conversation toward the task instead of letting the children guide their conversation. Parents might be worried about safety and may say things like, "Don't touch the pony. Don't climb inside the fence!" A teacher might say, "Here is one carrot. You can give them only one each." Although these are all important ideas to convey, the key is to be able to get your message across without limiting the social interaction among the children.

The following example takes place at a New England preschool located within an apple orchard farm. We find this setting to be one of the best places to facilitate socialization. Children show their enthusiasm for the animals, and they feel part of a community when they interact with what is around them. As Ann helps them interact, they talk together and become a likable, cohesive group.

In order to bring the environment into the conversation in a positive instead of limiting way, we've found that it's helpful to engage in a conversation that talks about friendship. In this example, Ann is talking to three preschool girls, all aged three. She is not only identifying the children's emotions and following their ideas, but teaching them to observe what friends do in real life. She took the opportunity to talk about friendship as they were looking at Tristan the pony and Angel the donkey:

ANN: Look at the leaves that are falling! Look at the leaves in the wind! (I point up toward the tree. The morning light is showing through the leaves. The colors are bright.)

MARISSA: Yeah! (Marissa points up toward the tree and looks at her peers.)

SAMANTHA: Because it's fall!

ANN: Isn't it beautiful!?

MARISSA: Uh-huh. (Marissa kicks up some red leaves.)

ANN: Wow! I wonder why the leaves fall off so fast!

MARISSA: Because it's fall!

ANN: Here comes Angel, the donkey. Tristan, come and get your carrots! (All three girls holler for the pony and the donkey. They run along the fence, watching each other, and waving a carrot.)

MARISSA: Samantha, will they eat it? Look, they're coming! They can see us! Tristan!

ANN: Hi, Tristan! Look at his face! Do you want to pet his nose? Just hold it [the carrot] out. Is it a little scary?

SAMANTHA: No. It's never scary for us!

ANN: Look, he has fuzzy ears!

MARISSA: He's crunching the carrots.

ANN: Look, they ate the whole bag of carrots. Look at Tristan's belly. It's all white. Do you think they're friends?

MARISSA: Oh, yeah, they are. They are!

ANN: One of the kids thought they were gonna get married because they were so happy!

MARISSA: Yeah, I think so!

ANN: Do you think they play a lot like friends?

SAMANTHA: Uh-mmm. (Yes!)

ANN: How can you tell if they're friends, Carly?

CARLY: Because they run together!

ANN: What else do they do because they're friends?

CARLY: They shake their tails together.

ANN: They shake their tails together. What else do they do?

CARLY: They do all the stuff that they want to!

ANN: They do all the stuff that they want to. They look at each other. Look. They put their noses together?

MARISSA: Uh-mmm. (She nods her head to mean yes.)

ANN: Just like friends. Do you think they talk to each other?

CARLY: No, they can't! (All three children laugh.)

ANN: They can't talk, but they can show each other by looking. Right?

CARLY: Uh-hmm. (All three girls hold hands and nod their heads in agreement. They run along the side of the pasture back to their preschool classroom. They talk and giggle to each other all the way back through the field.)

This outdoor setting also gives children an opportunity to look at something in the greater world that is related to their own life. They see how much they like each other as they share. Later, when the children enter the classroom and explain their adventure in the pasture, the entire class laughs with them, watches them, and listens. The whole class smiles and giggles as they tell their story, and the three girls are perceived as well liked.

Use the Environment to Teach Abstract Concepts During Play

The environment can also be used to help children understand an abstract concept, like the five senses or the difference between big and small. A child will remember an event that is meaningful to him, and if the event is associated with a concept, he'll understand the concept more than if he were looking at a photo in a book or listening to a teacher read a text. That's why parents and teachers need to look for opportunities in the child's environment that are meaningful to him.

This next dialogue occurred when Ann was on a walk with a group of children at a preschool. During the walk, she pointed out some cherry trees that the children had been watching grow since they were saplings. The children are invested in these trees, and Ann takes the opportunity to explain the concept of big versus small:

ANN: You think they look like cherry trees? Farmer Joe is planting them. Maybe they are different. Let's see. This tag is attached to the tree. It says "eastern red bud tree," and it says it will have . . . pink flowers . . . Listen to this: "pink flowers with heart-shaped leaves." That sounds beautiful.

MISSY: Ooh. It's going to be beautiful.

ANN: Oh, you are so right. This one is a yoshino cherry tree. A white-flowering cherry tree. You can find this type of tree in Washington, D.C., where the president lives.

CLAUDIA: Is this pollen too?

ANN: No, but I think it probably has pollen inside it. Because you see this part right here; I think the pollen is right in here.

CLAUDIA: Don't even think about smelling it.

ANN: Do you think these trees look similar?

CHILDREN: Yeah.

ANN: I do too. Oh yes, look at this: it says how big it is going to grow. It says it's going to grow between six and seven feet. Now six feet is right here. So it is going to be that tall or one more foot. That means if I put a ruler on top of where my hand is, to about there, that is the tallest it will be. That tree will be a giant tree. Do you see another tree it might be smaller than?

CLAUDIA: That one.

ANN: Yeah, I think it would be smaller than this one.

CLAUDIA: Those ones?

ANN: Definitely. Those pine trees there are smaller.

Several days later, Ann was walking with a preschooler from this group by the duck pond. The child said to her, "This duck is really tall with the feather on top of his head. He is swimming next to that duck, and he is short. He doesn't have a feather." She was able to show that she understood the abstract idea of big versus small and transfer the concept to a totally different medium: the ducks.

Combine the Environment with Play to Teach Sequencing

Children between ages three and five are struggling to formulate their ideas with language. They are learning to express their thoughts logically about what they want to share with peers and adults. At first, a child of two or three years uses language to request and protest.

Children will say, "I don't want that," or "I want that," or "I like that." This is the beginning level of communication. By four years of age, they start relating their ideas and their opinions. By age five, they start giving their strong opinions and sometimes insist that their ideas are more important than those of others. In order to make this transition, they have to learn how present their ideas and thoughts in a logical order or sequence. They also need to practice formulating their ideas with words to create intelligible sentences. This leads to being able to tell a story or explain an idea in logical order, which we call *sequencing*. Parents and teachers can use the environment as a tool for helping their child practice sequencing as early as the age of three. We have found that it will help children to use logic and sequencing not only in their words within sentences but with organizing their ideas when they try to tell stories.

The child is practicing a skill called *retelling*. An adult who is an active listener will respond back with comments and reinforce his explanation about what he sees or what is happening. When a teacher asks, "What did you do over summer vacation?" the child can explain and use his more complex vocabulary words. If the child is excited about his experience, such as going to a farm or a park or a swimming pool, he will be even more motivated to use more descriptive words and to retell the event clearly so he can share his excitement with his listener.

Preschoolers love to retell events about their life, and they respond to praise when a parent responds with enthusiasm and tells them, "Wow! That must have been a great experience!" Using the skills of sequencing thoughts or retelling an event indirectly increases a child's vocabulary and is essential for academic learning.

Three year olds can handle short sequences and retelling of one or two or three steps. In order to initiate this experience, choose something that requires the sequencing of thoughts. Some of our favorite projects are planting seeds in pots or teaching how to mix colors. For example, Ann was once showing a group of three year olds how to plant a seed. Because each was holding an empty flower pot, she said that first they put in some dirt and then they put in the seed. Next, the children were to add more dirt over the seed to keep it warm, and then cover the dirt with water. The three year olds could repeat and perform the three steps, but it was hard for them to remember why they were doing the project. Ann had to remind them repeatedly that the fourth step was that the plant would grow.

With four or five year olds, you can work with experiences that are more abstract. Retelling real events encourages social engagement in five year olds as they begin to talk to each other about what they did the day before or over the weekend. If they can't describe and retell, they can't answer a peer's question. Children also need to be able to describe and retell what they are doing in a play sequence, which keeps the conversation going.

The next phase is moving from retelling to a peer to the ability to create a new story with a peer. A child can make a social connection by joining another child to tell a pretend or actual story. The story could include an orientation, a theme, characters, actions, a high point or exciting moment, and an ending, but not necessarily in this order. Research on a diversity of cultures has shown that the way families tell stories at home can differ in narrative structure and sequence and influence how children tell their stories to their friends or teachers. Some families begin with the exciting high point of a story, while other families don't sequence events in their stories. In some cultures, families learn to sequence their ideas following their culture's storytelling rules. Teacher expectations must vary for each child's culture and take into account what children have learned or heard at the dinner table at home.

In this next excerpt, Ann is listening to a four year old describe how he built a boat out of blocks. The pretend boat was created out of blocks to represent the wood hull of the boat, real cardboard to represent the rigging of the boat, and pieces of left-over scrap paper that was part of the boat's cabin. He also created a pretend environment of water, a harbor, and a sandy beach that all became part of his imaginary play. Ann helps the boy logically organize his thinking between the real world of his boat that he saw in a pond near his house and his imaginary environment that he created at school. Here he tries to describe his project:

ANN: Marty, tell how you organized this whole thing of blocks. It's so cool!

MARTY: Well it's sort of a creation.

ANN: So, what's this?

MARTY: The switches. (Marty points to blocks indicating that they should move the boat along different parts of the water, like channels or canals.)

ANN: That's neat. I like that thing in the back (pointing to the towers on the pretend police boat). So how did you start this whole thing? Did you think of it in your mind as you were building it?

MARTY: Umm, it wasn't that. Just building it.

ANN: I like the way you made it. How did you organize this part?

MARTY: We got the scrap metal.

ANN: Oh, there was some scrap metal on the dock, and you built this part?

MARTY: Yeah.

ANN: Cool. How did you build these? These are like out of wood, huh?

MARTY: Actually they're special metal.

ANN: They look like switches.

MARTY: The switches are on here. You have to pull really hard because it's really tough to get them. (Marty is pretending that he has switches in his hands by holding on to two long blocks and struggles as he pulls them down.)

ANN: It's tough to get them?

MARTY: You, umm, can't whack 'em over. (He smacks his hand over the switches.)

ANN: Oh, I see. You have set them up really strong so the waves can't knock them down?

MARTY: Well, this is the lever to go.

ANN: The lever to go into stop. Yeah.

MARTY: Right now it's stop. This is go. All the way down.

ANN: All the way down is go. Oh, that's neat. That's your steering. That's so cool. I like the way you have your seat organized too. So when you're building this, do you think about it as you build? You sort of visualize it in your mind what it's going to be like?

MARTY: Actually, it's not really.

ANN: Not really. You just build it.

MARTY: I just build it. We have directions of how to build the hull so it doesn't sink.

ANN: Oh. How do you get those directions?

MARTY: We put them . . . we just have known in the past how to do it.

ANN: So you know from the past. Oh.

MARTY: So, in case we forget.

ANN: So, experience is what does it. Right? Your experience?

MARTY: Uh-hum. Yeah.

ANN: So if you've done it before, you know how to build it.

MARTY: Yeah, how to build the hull and stuff.

ANN: Wow! That must be exciting. It's a great boat. It's the best pretend boat I've ever seen.

Notice how the conversation begins with Ann asking questions, such as, "How did you organize this whole thing?" Then Ann asks if he visualized the boat before he built it or if he just thought about it as he created it. Marty responds, "I just build it." In order to continue the sequence of his thoughts, Ann asks for further details about his thinking: how he got these directions to build the hull of the boat. He answers with a logical reason: "We've known in the past how to do it." Ann names this as "experience," and he agrees that he remembers how to build a boat from his experience.

The story sequence is becoming clear. When he mentions that he has some "scrap metal," Ann asks for more details. When he attempts to describe how the water is pushed aside as the boat moves ahead, Ann helps him rephrase how he describes this process. At this point in his story sequence, he is smiling. He is pleased that he is understood and that Ann is excited about his wonderful boat project. His face lights up with pride. He moves around his boat, dancing from one end to the other, pointing out how the wave is created by his boat moving fast. He makes the sounds of the wave.

Finally, he announces that the boat has traveled to another shore. The story ends here, and Ann compliments him and thanks him. He runs up to the bow of the pretend boat, and invites his classmates by saying, "All aboard!" They run to join Marty. He organizes where each classmate will sit. He becomes the captain of his own ship. He makes the sounds of a ship moving out to sea, a foghorn blows, and he is off to another imaginary land with his crew.

TIPS FOR FACILITATING PLAY

Each of the following techniques will help ensure that your child gets the most out of her interactions with you and the environment. The key is that all of these strategies involve you; your child cannot become an advanced, successful child alone. It's not just the content of the dialogues that makes for a successful child, but how you deliver your role in each of these interactions.

Hand Out the Compliments

Preschoolers usually respond positively to praise, regardless of whether it comes from an adult or a peer. They are thrilled to receive a compliment about what they made or are building. When Ann complimented Matt on his "cool" boat, he responded with a smile, and his face was beaming with pride. More important, Ann's positive words encouraged Matt to keep building and to keep describing his project. The praise kept him loose and talkative because he knew he was doing a good job, and he was being rewarded by Ann's praise and her attention.

Repeat the Stories with the Same Words and Emotion

Parents and teachers need to listen to the child's language and then rephrase, using the same emotion, the details of what the child is saying. By rephrasing the child's language, a parent is making it clear to the child that he has been heard and also that the parent feels what the child feels about the situation. The parent's rephrasing doesn't need to be exact, but the parent must use the identical voice intonation pattern, gesture, and body language that accompanied the child's explanation. This sensitive and emotional response to a child's story is another form of praise, showing that you agree with what is being said and identifying it as important and meaningful. As the child hears more of the parent's rephrasing of his language and feels the parent's response, he'll gain confidence and want to engage more with his peers. You're making a connection with your child, and he will want to make this same kind of sensitive connection with others.

Speak Clearly and Calmly

Preschoolers love to imitate voice patterns, which is why it is so important to model an appropriate loudness, pitch, and cadence of speaking. Use a calm, steady voice that is not too fast or too loud. When a child uses the right intonation pattern and tone of voice and volume, he will be heard by his peers and other adults. A child who can talk clearly and at an appropriate level will be viewed as kind, caring, and more advanced than the child who does not possess this skill.

Speak from the Heart

Preschoolers respond directly to honest social affect. They will pick up on the frustration, disappointment, or joy in a parent's tone, volume, facial expressions, gestures, and body language. What's more, they'll use it in their own conversations. So when you are speaking with your preschooler, respond with genuine affect, gesture, and body language. If you respond with disingenuous affect that appears to be too theatrical, you will be rejected by your child or his peers. This is true even with children who are experiencing language delays and have not learned to use language to express their own genuine emotions. They are often perceived to be more "insensitive" to the subtleties of language, but in reality they are often very attuned. When children receive a genuine emotional response from an adult or a peer, they are moved and will respond with real emotion. This is what entices a child to use reciprocal engagement and become socially engaged. He believes that you are really hearing and seeing how he feels. He feels the relationship because it is real.

With practice, your child will pick up all of the skills and make them her own. A child who is familiar with how to read subtle language cues, can modulate her voice and get her point across, and can accept a compliment with grace will be viewed by others as successful. By using the environment as a tool for facilitated play and by becoming involved directly in that play, you are giving your child the opportunity to get the most out of every day.

These tools will help your child see the perspective of others and be able to negotiate not only her wants and desires but those of her friends. Teachers admire these skills, which then leads to more praise for the child who will develop with more self-confidence.

IN SUMMARY

- Play fosters an impressive array of skills that are necessary for children's academic and social success.
- Free play and choice time give children access to practice relating to peers.
- The outdoor environment helps a child not only grasp language but also connect to the perspectives of others.

CHAPTER FOUR

Ensuring a Happy Child

HAPPINESS IS JUST AS ELUSIVE for children as it is for adults. While parents don't expect their children to be happy all of the time, they do want their children to be happy at least most of the time. But what do we mean by "happiness"? And can we recognize when our children are truly happy? Does happiness look the same for everyone?

This chapter will teach you how to help your child regulate her emotions, become more content with social interactions, and develop a sense of confidence and happiness with others.

We've learned from our clinical and educational work that what is happiness for some is misery for others. A preschooler may show delight by smiling, jumping up and down, waving his arms upward, and telling his peers that he likes what they are doing, thinking, or feeling. Or he might just shout out his feelings. Once Ann watched a preschooler jumping off a log in the middle of the play area, yelling, "I'm happy! I love jumping!" As she landed, she laughed until she rolled over in the grass, clutching her waist, and shouting, "I'm so happy!"

Other preschoolers may show their happy feelings when they are quiet and playing by themselves, building, drawing, or creating an imaginative story. They may want to share their story or construction and will bring another child over to see it, and then they might show their happiness when they respond to their peer's compliment.

When this happens, they may show a slight smile, and sometimes lean into the friend and giggle or pat her on the shoulder.

Other children may never show their happiness, and yet when they are asked, they will agree that they are happy. Some children go as far as to disguise their happiness because they want to enjoy being content alone.

Many factors influence how a child displays happiness. Most children learn from an embedded family culture that values certain emotional expressions. For example, in some cultures, a child is not expected to show happiness and is asked to be quiet or even silent during times that would be cause for raucous displays of delight in other cultures. In addition, the child's state of mind, feeling of pressure to perform in school or in the household, or feelings of insecurity that her sibling is "better" all affect her own happiness and how and when she displays this emotion.

Despite these family differences, happiness should include a feeling that all (or most) is right with the particular family culture and the world, and that each individual understands her added value to the bigger picture. A child feels happy when she feels connected to the significant people in her life. This social experience builds positive feelings of trust, security, and self-confidence.

WHEN CHILDREN ARE HAPPY

Preschoolers are happy when they please their teachers and parents. They enjoy fixing things that are broken, rallying around a friend on the playground, helping a teacher carry a library book, or working with mom or dad in the kitchen. When three to five year olds are asked what really makes them happy, they usually respond with something like, "Having fun playing." Susan Miller, author of "Helping Happiness Along," says, "Simply being engaged in active outdoor play with friends seems to be a favorite event that brings preschoolers great happiness."[1] But how can we ensure that children enter a happy brain state and play with confidence?

The Importance of Make-Believe Play

Researchers note that make-believe play is the primary socialization experience that contributes to an emotionally well-regulated and happy child. According to Laura Berk and her colleagues, children learn to self-regulate their emotions by using cognitive strategies to control emotions and impulses and to act according to moral standards, monitoring thinking and behavior in pursuit of expectations of others and their own goals.[2] This thinking process is apparent in the early months of life as children learn to deal with arousal and modulation of sensory stimulation. Yet it is not until the preschool years that they really start to control emotions and impulses. The Berk studies also found that make-believe play strengthens the ability of a child who is at risk for developmental delays in play and speech to self-regulate.

Teachers and parents can help a child with self-regulation by developing dramatic play stories where conflicts are resolved. Through these experiences, the child learns the correct language to use that is acceptable to peers, as well as the self-soothing skills to calm his own emotions as he plays. He sees what controls the emotions of his peers and sees as well the expectations of others and responds to these demands during imaginative play.

Private Speech

Preschoolers use what clinicians call *private speech*: a tool where the child talks to herself aloud about what she's thinking. This private speech is absolutely normal and accounts for 20 to 60 percent of children's language utterances during play.[3] According to Berk and her colleagues, children using private speech are taking over support provided by others. Preschoolers are working through their own ideas and making self-guiding comments for the tasks that are most challenging. Children who use private speech are seen as more regulated than their peers in play. That is, they are able to guide their own challenges and control their own emotions and think about what language they are using to meet the expectations of others.

Children integrate private speech dialogues by using a rich tapestry of voices learned from their social world. This self-engagement brings into their play the values, strategies, and a skill learned from parents and teachers and provides a way for children to work through their own ideas. Berk found that during this type of pretend play, each child is learning how to manage intense emotions and master social skills. She also noted that children who use private speech during play become more attentive and involved, and they perform better than their less talkative peers.[4] Researcher N. Y. Broderick, found that four to five years olds judged by teachers as using more private speech during free play and during art and puzzle activities were rated as more self-regulated than classmates who didn't use as much private speech. They were more attentive to their tasks.[5] At the same time, they become better at self-regulating during play, which leads directly to a happy, content state and a sense that they are in control.

We've also found that the happiest children are those who have a strong sense of self and a sense of humor, and they become personally involved in their play. They use a mixture of private speech and talking to their peers in a continual dialogue about their feelings. They love to play with others as well as by themselves. They are confident in the person they are, even at their young age.

Parents and teachers can contribute to a child's feeling of happiness by supporting her during play, praising her, and helping her make connections between her emotions and using language to express her ideas and opinions. These are the tools children need to create friendships and bring out positive aspects of their innate personalities so that they will seem happier to others.

THE SOURCES OF HAPPINESS

A child's emotional adjustment with peers and happiness in play is dependent on his ability to self-regulate his behavior and emotions, as well as his ability to organize his play experiences. Current studies are looking more closely at the biology of self-regulation. Studies linking the relationship between brain functioning and behavior are now suggesting that changes in the cerebral cortex, especially the frontal lobes, underlie gains in self-regulation.[6]

The Plasticity of the Brain

Researchers are looking at brain plasticity and how changes in the brain cause brain impulses to redirect into new pathways. Clinicians are using the new brain science research for their work with young children. Torkel Klingberg, a neuroscientist and author of *The Overflowing Brain*, discussed brain plasticity at a recent conference at MIT. He stated that "all types of experience and learning modify the brain."[7] His research uses functional magnetic resonance imaging tools and has uncovered how the brain changes when it is deprived of information. For example, when a person loses a limb, the corresponding part of the sensory cortex no longer receives information from that part of the body. However, the surrounding areas of the brain will start to fill in the space with neuron connections that relate to use of a limb.

These studies are still in progress, but they strongly suggest that the brain is constantly changing and that training may be an important part of this process. This research has implications for helping preschool children learn the language, self-regulation, and social cognitive skills involved in play.

This plasticity is one way that children gain self-regulation. Researchers, including C. A. Nelson, have found that the formation of synapses in the frontal lobes peaks during the preschool years and nearly doubles the adult number by around four years of age.[8] Afterward, the brain undergoes a period of synaptic pruning; during this time, neurological development that signifies a period of high plasticity or readiness for learning occurs. There is now evidence that self-regulation and higher cognitive function result from the dynamic interchange between brain activity and learned experiences.

This means that children learn from the examples set for them by others: teachers, parents, and peers.

High-Reactive Children

Harvard psychology professor Jerome Kagan is conducting a twenty-year longitudinal study of childhood behaviors related to brain function. He has found children who show signs of an easily aroused brain to the unfamiliar as early as four months of age. These infants, called "high reactive," thrash their arms and legs and may cry in the presence of continually moving objects that are unfamiliar. He believes that roughly 15 percent of children are highly reactive.[9]

Some of these temperamentally inhibited children may learn to compensate for their reactions, while others do not. According to Kagan's research, by adolescence, some of the children who exhibited these behaviors as infants were able to change their behaviors within supportive environments. For example, Kagan's study shows that high-reactive babies who went to day care when they were young were significantly less fearful at age four years than high reactives who stayed home. This doesn't mean that parents are poor child care providers, but it may suggest that children who are exposed to peers in a busy day care environment may learn from their exposure to other children to quiet their overly reactive brains and cope with the unfamiliar. They were able to learn to deal with stress and move toward a happier, more contented state. A child who is mostly at home may not need to cope and consequently does not learn to quiet her brain.

The child who can cope with an ever-changing world and roll with the waves of unpredictable moments in school usually reaches some state of happiness early in life. Even if a child is born with a tendency to be anxious when confronted with the unfamiliar, she may learn to cope and change her behavior and reactions. Therefore, the importance of play, socialization with caregivers, and parental involvement may lead to lasting positive changes within the brain.

Self-Regulation

Children who continue to experience poor self-regulation may eventually experience feelings of unworthiness or even childhood depression. However, we have found that even these children can change their behavior on their own, although some may need properly administered medications.

Some children may never become ebullient or bubbly, but they can become content and eager to relate socially to their peers. They can learn how to overcome their anxieties and relax around other children so that they can enjoy being in unfamiliar situations. Others will learn how to use language to engage in social interactions and express their own thoughts and feelings. Of course, children may always experience feelings of insecurity and a high-reactive temperament from time to time. But when they learn self-control and master an awareness to reframe certain sensations that trigger anxiety, they will be able to achieve a more relaxed, content mind.

The following examples help define what we mean by a child who can self-regulate and establish socially happy friendships during the preschool years. In order for this type of development to occur, children need to play with other children in unstructured time so they can think, work through their own ideas, talk to themselves, and be involved with peers. Yet at the same time, all children bring their own particular brain state to the play experience, and they will be at different ability levels in terms of coping with the reactions of others. They may need help from an adult in order for them to self-regulate their emotions and feelings.

Happy Children Connect Their Emotions with Language

Most interactive conversations are actually exercises in the use of *reciprocal language*, that is, the back-and-forth exchange of talk, gestures, body language, voice tone, facial expressions, and social affect.

A happy preschooler can engage in reciprocal language with his peers when he shares his own ideas or opinions. This child can read others' subtle cues of language, read facial expressions, watch body language and gestures, and predict how his peers are feeling and self-regulate his own state of emotions. With this understanding, part of the skill involved in perspective taking and understanding others, he is relating and connecting to peers. He can identify when a peer is being mean, or disappointing him, or even when he is excited about something. His peer is delighted when he acknowledges how he feels and tells him that he understands his thinking.

As children learn this skill, they make more social connections, which helps them to become happy. Even the shyest preschoolers love to have friends. Through these interactions, children get positive feed-back and feel valuable with peers.

Adults can encourage reciprocal language by engaging children in conversation and play. Stay at the child's eye level, responding to the conversation with your own facial expressions and gestures, and use body language that shows that you understand how the child feels. If you are engaging with two children, sit at the point of an imaginary triangle with the children equally spaced and facing you. If there are three children playing, create an imaginary rectangle in the same physical proximity. When they move, move with them, keeping the same distance. Position yourself so that you are not closer to one child or the other.

Within these physical dynamics, use facial expressions and body language with gesture to respond immediately to each child and allow them to read your language cues. Experiment with the way that your tone of voice and facial expression can change the meaning of what is being said.

Reciprocal Language

In the following dialogue, Ann is talking with two boys who are work-ing through their fear of bees. They are interacting with reciprocal lan-guage, talking back and forth with some sense of urgency. Notice that after every comment by one child, Ann uses affect, facial expression, and tone to encourage the boys to keep talking. She laughs, makes eye contact, and giggles. These cues show the boys that she is enjoying their conversation and, in addition, is supporting their own self-regulation around a sensitive subject: getting stung by a bee. The result is that the boys continue to interact: they're comfortable with each other instead of wary. They're involved, feeling a sense of control, regulating their own emotions, and happy.

SAM: (He begins to look surprised and twists his body.)

ANN: (Ann notices his body language.) That looks like a bee! A bumblebee!

REUBEN: But if you leave it alone, it won't sting you. Right? (Reuben shivers and winces.)

ANN: If you sit still. Right? Maybe that's it. (Ann looks around for the bee with body language and a facial expression that show a sense of urgency in her voice tone and imitates Reuben's shivering.) I don't like bees either.

REUBEN: I like bees. (Reuben changes his tone of voice.)

ANN: You do? I run when I see bees! (Ann uses a facial expression of fear.)

REUBEN: But, but . . . but, if you touch them first, it will sting you!

ANN: Yeah. (Ann looks at both boys and shakes her head to indicate that she supports his new idea.) I don't think I'd touch a bee.

REUBEN: Me either!

ANN: (Ann clenches her fists and holds her arms by her side and uses a facial expression of fear.) I'd be afraid. Wouldn't you? (Ann turns to Sam. He nods his head to say yes. Ann nods her head to say yes.)

REUBEN: I'm not afraid of bees. Bugs just buzz around, but bees can sting you. (Private speech to self: "Well, maybe they can sting.")

ANN: Bugs just buzz around. Bees can go zap! (Ann taps the table as if she was a pretend bee. She smiles as she moves her hand fast like a bee.)

REUBEN: But they give you flowers! (shows facial expression of happiness)

ANN: Well, that's right. They give you flowers! (Ann validates Reuben's change from fear to contentment by using her positive tone of voice and a big smile.)

When parents and teachers talk to young children, they should describe their own thoughts by adding facial expressions, gestures, and body language. This encourages children to respond back with affect and to understand the connection between language and emotions. At the same time, the children recognize that their parent understands their feelings.

Praise Matters

A parent who praises a child is giving positive reinforcement that can potentially last a lifetime. One of the best ways to praise a child is not by constantly saying, "Great job!" which then becomes a rote answer instead of a well-earned reward. A more subtle and effective approach is to rephrase what the child says during play, thereby letting the child know that you are supporting her ideas and opinions.

In the following example, two four-year-old preschool girls are drawing on their hands with markers. They insist that drawing on hands is acceptable. A typical response by a parent or a teacher might be to tell the children to stop and wash their hands immediately, without even asking why the children were drawing on their hands in the first place. The children may then feel bad about their behavior. Worse, they'll stop using language to explain their opinion and ideas.

Instead, Ann chose to let the girls explain their reasons for drawing on their hands. She then praises the girls for talking openly about their ideas. This practice reduces anxiety for the children as they become more comfortable with the skill of retelling ideas. At the same time, Ann is making sure that the girls understand the concept of cause and effect. Preschoolers need practice in explaining the reasons that something happens or the cause and effect of their own actions. If they wash with water and soap, the drawing will come off their hands.

In addition, Ann asks them short and direct questions to help them sequence their ideas about what happened. This is called *scaffolding*, or guiding them through the thinking process, and it helps children continue to talk and make connections between the words they use and their actions in play. Scaffolding allows children to feel more confident and want to talk more about their opinions.

ANN: Show me your hands. (Both girls extend their arms outward. Both arms have marker drawings on them.)

ANN: What have you been doing?

AMY: We've been . . .

NATALIE: . . . drawing.

ANN: Oh, you've been drawing. (Ann laughs.) Do you always draw on your hands?

AMY: Yeah. (Natalie also nods her head to say yes.)

ANN: Well, what about the paper?

AMY: Ah, well, we already did that.

ANN: And you got tired of the paper.

AMY: Yeah.

ANN: So you decided to draw on yourself?

AMY: Yeah.

ANN: What does your mommy tell you when you draw on your hands?

AMY AND NATALIE: Wash them.

ANN: Oh, you have to wash them. You think it will come off?

NATALIE: Yeah! It will come off with the water and the soap in the sink.

ANN: What if it wouldn't come off at all?

NATALIE: It would.

ANN: Then would you have your hands like that forever and ever?

NATALIE: Well, it's smooshed on.

ANN: It's really smooshed on. Well, it'll probably come off if you wash it. Can you give each other a high five with your painted hands? (Natalie and Amy smack their painted hand together and laugh.)

When Natalie and Amy express their delight in drawing on their hands and arms, they are serious and engaged with the listener. They are proud of their "art work" and want an adult to praise them. Amy knew from previous experience that the marker will come off with water and soap. As Ann responds with positive affect, both children realized that they might have to work hard to get the "smooshed" marker off their arms, but as long as she wasn't angry, they were pleased.

The result of this exchange is that both children continue to use expressive speech and logical reasoning skills. They laugh and smack their hands together at the end to announce that they are having fun. The reward in this situation is a positive experience and a happy connection.

Parents and teachers can use this same scaffolding in their own interactions with children, even when they might not be pleased with an outcome at first. They should continue to show positive affect and limit negative body language that might indicate that the children are "in trouble."

Happy Children Can Keep Play Going

Five year olds can create complicated stories. They either include others or want to be in control of the story and play alone. While they laugh, run, and talk at the same time, they never forget their story, even if several children are playing with them. Within the story, children will express their own opinions and ideas, and because they are free to do so, they are content and happy. They stay connected with their playmates for the duration of the game.

Parents can help children keep stories going by allowing the children to direct their play. One early morning at a preschool, Ann was watching a group of five year olds, mostly girls, dance together inside a gazebo. Each held a thin stick, and they were laughing, obviously happy. The tallest girl, whose long, blonde hair was swinging across her back, danced out of the gazebo with confidence, waving her "wand." Ann supported their ideas in their story, which focused on the girls' creating their own rules that would deal with their emotional reactions to the problems they perceive in the world:

SHARON: I'm the head fairy. Would you like to come into our fairy house?

ANN: Of course! But what are the rules?

SHARON: Oh, here are the rules. We made them up! (Sharon, the head fairy and rule maker, waves her wand with each rule.) First, we tap everything that is bad with our stick to make it good. Then we tap everything that is dead to make it live. Then we tap the air and the trees and anything around us to make the world more peaceful, because the world is in trouble!

ANN: Wow. You have very special rules. I like your rules. Can I play?

SHARON: Sure. (She runs out of the gazebo with the other girls following her, each waving her wand.)

ANN: (Following them with a wand, Ann notices that they are tapping the shoulders of their classmates, but only the boys.) Why are you tapping all the boys? To make them good?

SHARON: Yes, because boys are basically bad.

ANN: Do you believe that boys are really bad?

SHARON: No, this is only pretend. But sometimes boys can be rough.

Young children often express their worries through play. They talk about the world they have been exposed to through the media and from listening to adults. They also know that their classmates enjoy pretend games that involve killing and fighting as they act out the stories they hear about war. As adults, we can help children understand their world through play by encouraging and supporting their stories, either real or pretend.

A child who expresses that the world needs to be fixed, as Sharon did, needs support and someone to hear her concerns. Her feelings need to be validated. One way to do this is to join the conversation, name what the child is feeling and talking about, and encourage the child to keep talking in order to move the story to a reasonable end.

A parent can also have a discussion about what the child was thinking once play is over and the child's narrative has ended.

A child's engagement in pretend play with friends is linked to a wide range of favorable skills such as language development, understanding emotions, understanding the perspectives of others, and social competence. Since self-regulation is the main skill needed in pretend play and is indicative of social and cognitive maturity, make-believe play contributes to these important outcomes for a preschool child.

Happy Children Make Friends by Making Others Happy

Many children need help in learning how to stay with a peer and keep their friend happy as they play. In the following interaction, two fast-moving five year olds, Billy and Harrison, are playing on the playground but with separate agendas. Billy is carrying a GI Joe, and Harrison is wearing a Batman costume and trying to climb the bars to pretend to fly. Neither Billy nor Harrison is noticing what the other is doing even though they are next to each other. The boys are clearly involved in their own play ideas. Each wants his friend to join in, but neither child wants to give up his personal play story.

In this situation, a parent or a teacher might try to physically keep Harrison and Billy apart. Or they might try redirecting the boys by eliminating one theme. Typically parents might say, "Harrison, you can fly later!" or say, "Billy is so disappointed. He wants you to play with him! Look at him."

Instead parents should engage the peers together. You'll see that Ann validates Harrison's ideas and praises his play agendas. She stays at his eye level, reinforcing the idea that an adult likes what he is doing. Using gestures and an enthusiastic voice tone, Ann asks Harrison to notice his friend, Billy. Harrison glances over at Billy, and Ann runs over to kneel down near Billy. Harrison watches Ann move toward his friend. With affect and body language (kneeling near the child, joining the child in his play space area, pointing to the shared object, GI Joe, using eye contact), Ann engages in conversation with Billy and eventually gets the two boys to become involved with each other instead of parallel playing.

ANN: Hi! What are you doing?

HARRISON: Doing monkey bars!

ANN: What's your costume?

HARRISON: (He pats his chest and smiles.) Batman.

ANN: That's cool. Are you flying across those monkey bars?

HARRISON: Yep. I'm pretending I was on a big building that was cracked open and I was climbing on them.

ANN: A big building that cracked open and you were climbing on it? Hey, Billy, where's Harrison? (He continues to fix GI Joe, but he looks up at the bars and points to Harrison.) Right here!

HARRISON: Right here! (Billy and Harrison run to get on a big plastic rocking dragon on the playground. They sit close to each other and laugh.) This is just what I like to see! (Billy sits right behind him on the dragon as they both start to rock back and forth.)

ANN: Hey, you guys. What are you doing?

HARRISON: We're riding on my pet dragon. (They both rock back and forth on the dragon. Harrison is in front holding the bar around the dragon's neck like a rein.)

ANN: Where's he going?

HARRISON: He's going to cycle riding!

BILLY: (Jumps off the dragon and follows his friend, smiling. The boys continue to play on several structures on the playground for the next twenty minutes without leaving each other.)

Parents and teachers may need to make simple suggestions or create a new idea for two children to connect their play themes. In this example, Ann helped Harrison think about where he is riding and what he is doing. When his friend joins him, she encourages them by asking them where they are riding. Harrison responded, and they were off to play for over twenty minutes.

A Happy Child Enjoys Helping Others

Preschoolers love to be helpers. It makes them feel happy to know that they are pleasing their parents or teachers. They love to find things for their friends and develop a level of satisfaction when they make a tangible contribution.

A happy child looks for opportunities to help classmates. For example, Ann was once working with Oliver, a four-year-old preschooler. Oliver was spinning a small merry-go-round on the playground that was packed with other four years olds. He was clutching the bars around the platform, running, trying to increase the speed of the merry-go-round. The other children were clinging to the bars that were within reach, but as the merry-go-round turned faster, the children fell to the ground. Some were in tears, and others were busy dusting off sand.

Oliver immediately recognized that he was going too fast, stopped spinning the merry-go-round, and rushed to help each child. He brushed off sand from a peer's jeans. He patted another on the head and said, "I'll help you up!" He smiled and encouraged them all to get back on the merry-go-round and to sit in the center so they wouldn't fall again. On the next round, he created a "high-five" falling-down game, and his whole class tried to join him.

Oliver loves to be engaged at all times and create situations that he thinks are fun and will engage others. This is when he is happiest: when his friends are laughing and having fun. When I asked Oliver, "Why are you so happy?" he answered, "Oh, I like to help my friends out of trouble!" In other scenarios, Oliver tries to get his teachers to laugh with him, especially during a crisis. He always seems to find a way to turn moments of disaster into happy moments of joint play by helping children help each other.

Parents and teachers should encourage children to be helpful, even when it means additional work for them. However, instead of just asking a child to do something ("Can you hand me the chalk?"), make the request while pointing out the feelings you experience when you help others. Explain what accomplishment and pride feel like to you, and then link those thoughts to the child's actions—for example, "Can you get that book for me way over on that far table, next to the lamp? You know, I really enjoy helping you get on your coat: it makes me feel useful." After the child brings you the book, say, "Oh, that was so helpful. Thank you for going all the way around your classmates to get that book! I'm proud of you. Now I can read it to the whole class. They will love this book!"

Make a point of explaining that helping others is emotionally satisfying and part of the responsibility of being a citizen within a greater community, even if the community is your family. When your child feels that he is a valued participant in something larger than himself, he will develop more self-esteem and consequently will feel happy.

Sometimes the best teachers turn out to be peers. Although we can set our own examples of good behavior, preschoolers also learn from their friends. Engage a peer who is good at helping others. Show your own genuine emotional response to her positive drive to help another person. Then watch your child take in this information. Afterward, ask your child how she felt and determine if she connected her peers' happiness with her own engagement of helping others.

TIPS FOR CREATING A HAPPY ENVIRONMENT

The following strategies can help parents and teachers not only assist their children, but also to help them be more present in young children's lives: to show their children that they are important enough to listen to, to be with, and to be heard.

Identify Individual Differences in Children's Abilities to Create a Happy Moment

Respect your child's individual needs and need to self-regulate his own emotions and respond in a supportive way that validates how he feels. Some children are anxious, shy, or reticent.

These children need a more supportive approach from an adult; they may want to be cuddled or held, for example. However, some shy children require less physical contact, more predictable routines, and clear structure that sets up their play. Other children need peer models or adults to point out happiness in specific events. Children with special needs require extra visuals, prompting, praise, and perhaps reinforcement to develop a happy state. Remember that many preschool children are trying to please their parents, while others are challenging their parents. In the process of pleasing or challenging, children strive to be the person their parents expect them to be. By allowing them to find their own ways to express happiness, you are giving them the opportunity to uncover the person they truly are.

Use a Kind Tone of Voice to Promote an Easy-Going Nature During Play

Children read subtle cues from voice patterns, including rate of speech and volume. If you can use a relaxed tone of voice when you engage your child in play, you'll give the signal that you really want to play with her. If you use a demanding tone, spoken at a fast rate, your child will hear that she is being tested and respond in a less playful manner. Or if you speak too loudly when you are close to your child, the child will get the wrong message—perhaps the message that you are angry. Adults often use a stern intonation and are then surprised when the listener misunderstands their message. This voice pattern can influence the listener to think that the speaker is either angry or unhappy. One of the best ways to show a child kindness is to use a moderate, natural tone of voice that sends the signal that you are happy and content and want your child to be the same.

Use Short Questions or Suggestions to Allow Children to Sequence Their Ideas or Explain Their Opinions During Make-Believe Play

Preschoolers learn the difficult art of understanding the content of language through pretend play experiences. They have to draw inferences from words and transfer the thoughts of one person to the next response. In order to master this art of self-regulating their emotions and ideas, some children need concrete, simple questions to help them put their thoughts into logical order. This internal process allows them to master some of the skills of *social cognitive (receptive) language* in order to understand language structure. They need help organizing their thoughts and regulating their emotions as they talk. In order to practice language skills, particularly retelling events, take advantage of all the events your child attends or activities he is engaged in, such as building a tower with blocks or going apple picking with his class. Use direct questions that help him follow a sequence:

- What was it like?
- Did you get to do something special?
- Who was there?
- Tell me more. I like what you are telling me. How did you feel?
- Did you like it?
- Do you want to do that again?
- Was there a problem?
- How did you solve it?
- How did things end?

These types of questions, and the situation in which you are asking them, are quite different from the kinds of questions that you may use during play interactions. When you are asking a child to retell an event, you are supporting his logical reasoning. During play interactions, the goal is to engage the child in making additional comments and being reciprocal with language. There is a constant interplay between the speaker and the listener. Asking questions during play is productive, but the questions need to be timed so they don't interrupt the flow of the play sequence. During these times, you may need to stop asking questions, fade back, and narrate the actions of the play. But when talking about recent events, you're working to improve expressive speech and develop a child's language skills—the complex task of putting together words and language structure for expressing thoughts and feelings. Expressive speech and language is the way we link voice to meaning. Preschoolers not only struggle with formulating their words into the right grammatical structures; they also have to practice defining their own thoughts and feelings for themselves. This is not an easy process for preschoolers. If you allow them to hear your words when you narrate what you are doing together, instead of asking constant, pointed questions, you will more likely help them express their feelings.

Point Out the Humor in Everyday Life

Use affect and engage with children as you enjoy what you are doing with them. Show them specifically what is funny about a particular situation, event, or even a television show. Children will read your cues when you are happy and respond in kind. When a child points out something funny in a situation, rephrase it for him as well as for the whole group. Preschoolers also love to act out funny or happy situations with puppets or other visuals to show peers, which allows them to identify situations that are happy. Happy children love to create journals and draw pictures of what makes them happy, so these activities should be fostered as well. When something minor happens that could be upsetting to your child—for example, a structure that she is building falls over—it's best to respond either with humor or to find a new way to help the child re-create the project. Create a story about a superhero who rescues the whole building. Pretend with your child, and be silly. You and your child will start laughing, and she will learn to respond with less anxiety to the unpredictable. Instead, she will learn that humor is her ally.

These suggestions are meant to help your child feel less anxious as she learns to self-regulate her emotions. Ultimately she will feel better about herself.

By now, you should be able to understand the difference between a child who is quiet but happy and a child who is quiet and anxious. By having the tools to express themselves in a logical manner, many children can control the performance anxiety that sometimes accompanies the preschool experience. Then they can relax and connect with other children. These children are able to express how they feel in make-believe play, in play that mirrors the reality of life, and even in the bigger, societal picture, as they begin to frame their own moral development.

IN SUMMARY

- Parents and teachers can contribute to children's feelings of happiness by supporting them during play and praising them.
- Help your child by establishing a positive relationship that can point out the humor in everyday life.
- The happiest children want to help others.

CHAPTER FIVE

g *Strong*

haracter

NG to understand that we live
ble for following the social rules
nly by the geographical location
but our personal family legacy, ethnicity, and religious beliefs. These
cultural norms create the base of morality. Children with a strong
moral understanding realize when they are breaking these rules and
when others are not adhering to them. They can identify the difference between right and wrong and can recognize this difference while
playing with friends as well as parents and teachers.

This chapter will help you identify and define moral character. Children recognize and develop their own interpretation of
social and moral codes by observing and engaging in conversation
with their parents and other adults and by exposure to cultural
activities. Children learn to differentiate between good and bad, or
acceptable and unacceptable behavior, directly from adults in their
community and by playing with their peers, with or without adult
guidance.

WHAT BUILDS YOUR CHILD'S CHARACTER

We believe that parent-child and teacher-child interactions are some of the best ways that children learn moral development and the consequences of bad behavior. Research in parent-child interactions suggests that a child defines right versus wrong through the parent's use of the word *no* in relation to a particular action. This means that even the youngest child begins to understand what is right through negotiations with parents who define good and bad behavior, especially if they also demonstrate a distinct set of consequences for such actions.

Parents' Role in Developing a Child's Character

The way parents talk to their children influences how they will use language and develop their own moral code when they play with their friends. Harvard education professor Catherine Snow believes that the parents' role of promoting empathy begins in infancy as parents help their children learn by linking what is going on in real life with dialogue or pretend stories.[1] By talking with the child about degrees of badness or goodness in stories, parents can explore the reasons, rules, and consequences of particular situations. Snow's research has shown that at age two and a half, children talk about "bad things" in terms of limiting actions ("I don't do that. That's bad."), but the emphasis shifts to "good" concepts by age three and a half ("I'm being a good boy."). By the time they are between the ages of four and a half to six, children are switching their language to include "should" and "shouldn't" ("You shouldn't grab my toys because I won't like you. That's not a good idea.").

Stories shared between parents and children help children understand how morality is constructed. Parents can use these stories and create moral lessons by talking about different characters who exhibit the right or wrong behavior. The moral importance of the story is defined by the consequences that happen to someone in the story or to themselves or another child during a play interaction in real life. For example, many popular children's books are based on themes of morality. One example is Eric Carle's *Do You Want to Be My Friend?* In the book, a lonely mouse is looking for a friend and meets several unfriendly animals such as the alligator and the lion that are not "nice." The mouse finds the "just right friend" who is nice. Characters from *Winnie the Pooh* are also helpful. When Pooh's friends all come to help Pooh when he is stuck in the rabbit hole, they are exhibiting "good moral behavior" and taking care of each other.

Children also learn from their own actions and the actions of their peers. Once a three year old said to Ann, "My friend took my blue sled. I shouldn't grab it away from him because I would be bad. Right?"

Socialized children have a strong moral understanding and can follow the rules of the culture, relate to classmates, and become respected and connected in the community. Most parents agree that a child who adheres to a strong understanding of moral values is easier to be with, talk with, and include in social interactions.

The Influence of Culture

The cultural aspect of morality is defined by how we interact with each other and what activities are valued within the home, where children learn what aspects of life the family values. For example, in some families and their extended cultures, it is more important for a child to learn to draw and express ideas and emotions through the visual rather than through oral language. In other families, children are expected to use language to express their thoughts as well as their feelings and emotions. Other cultures combine oral language with a strong use of subtle language cues.

Ann was once working with a young preschool girl from Japan. Yumi's teachers thought that she was "pensive" and a sensitive child who rarely used language to express her emotions. Yumi didn't relate to or interact with the other children, and when she did, she would talk in a soft whisper. She loved to be alone, drawing circles over and over again on large pieces of paper. Her teachers were also concerned about this repetitive behavior and thought that she might be a candidate for an evaluation for autism.

Ann was called in as the consultant. When Ann arrived during recess, she noticed Yumi sitting near the fence, pointing to the ground. She looked up and smiled, and said, "It's the crocus. See? It's almost spring."

Yumi continued to explain the concept of the seasons in detail, a rather sophisticated and abstract concept for a three year old. Then Yumi led Ann into her classroom and showed off her drawings of several large and small circles on a large white piece of paper. When Ann asked about the circles, Yumi giggled and pointed to the drawing and said, "This is the universe, and these are the stars and the planets. See this is Saturn with rings, and this one is Jupiter."

After talking with her teachers, Ann found out that Yumi's parents were scientists, who often created scientific drawings with Yumi at home. Yumi was simply repeating an exercise that she loved to do with her family at home. Yumi didn't have autism or any disability. What's more, her language improved once her teachers realized that she was just recreating her family culture at school, concentrating on activities that her family valued. Yumi needed to relate to her home culture throughout the day in order to feel safe and accepted in school.

The Importance of Empathy

A second aspect to morality is mastering the concept of empathy: understanding and having compassion for the needs and feelings of others. In a *New York Times* article, Jane Brody writes that while the "capacity for empathy seems to be innate, and is evident in other species," the environment in which children are raised can "make a big difference in whether empathy is fostered or suppressed."[2] In order for children to feel empathy, Stanley Greenspan identifies that children need to recognize their own feelings and express them by labeling them and experiencing their emotions; then they will recognize the feelings of others.[3]

Cultural differences and parental choices can affect the way children perceive the need to be empathic. However, children cannot have a strong moral character without this skill. When they can truly understand and feel what another child, or even a parent, is thinking or feeling about a specific situation, they're able to understand the consequences of their own actions.

Children must learn that their behavior has a ripple effect: if it causes others to feel hurt, rejected, or defiant, the child needs to learn that this behavior has negative consequences. Children should also be able to recognize when they make others feel good about themselves. By the age of five, most children understand that a moral act is clarified by its consequences or by the cultural values of their family or community.

Empathy is also more fully understood when we have the language to convey our own feelings. Some cultures, including our own, suggest that parents or teachers who can imitate a child's actions can provide the best examples for children to discover another person's feelings. Parents can begin to interpret their child's emotions before the age of two, but they will see the greatest impact at ages three and four. What's more, children who hear their parents talk about feelings are more likely to talk about their own feelings. Research has revealed strong correlations between the amount of maternal talk about feelings to eighteen month olds and the same children's talk about their own inner states at twenty-four months.[4]

Being empathic does not necessarily mean that you are comfortable talking about other's emotions. For example, some cultures value the ability to discuss the feelings of others, while others don't feel that it is appropriate. The cultures that don't value conversations about feelings are no less empathic or less moral; they simply do not engage in that kind of conversation. For example, a famous study by New York University professor of anthropology Bambi B. Schieffelin and Elinor Ochs, professor of linguistics at University of Southern California, explains that language socialization of children draws not only on the language interaction from a culture, but the psychological and anthropological background of a family or a society. Schieffelin focused on children's language development within different cultures and found that in some societies, children acquire "different sets of understandings about communication with their caretakers."[5] For example, they documented that a child growing up in the Kaluli tribe, a culture found in the tropical rainforests of the Southern Highlands of Papua, New Guinea, was not expected to relate to others on an emotional level unless that person specifically tells him what he is thinking. In this culture, no individual holds power, and everyone has equal access to resources. Kaluli children are taught that the giving and receiving of food is a way to measure affection, and the sharing of food is the focus of social relations. These children can recognize negative behavior and understand how a negative action relates to negative consequences: bad behavior is punished by taking away food, which is then identified with loneliness.

Lying and Morality

Understanding the purpose of lying is one of the best ways that parents can determine if children understand morality and have developed a moral character. A lie can be a conscious attempt at manipulating others to get what you want. Sometimes lying is a form of getting attention or teasing so that the parent will see the child's sense of humor. Or a lie can be an unconscious mistake that happens within communication.

Some children who lie to manipulate know that they are breaking a rule because they're using language in a way that goes against the social rules or moral code of their community. Others don't care what others think about them when they lie, and others purposely lie to get something in return.

Children who have stable friendships display a more advanced understanding of lying than those who have no lasting friends.

And children who get caught telling lies or deceiving their peers on purpose, or who cannot recognize others' feelings, are not popular or successful in our culture.

Preschoolers can usually recognize a lie that is coming from their friends or the adults who frequently surround them. Even three year olds can identify when something said was deceptive or morally wrong. In one study in Australia, children ages three to five were able to correctly identify a deliberately false statement as a lie and an inadvertently false statement as a mistake. In this age group, children exceeded the level of accuracy that would be expected by chance in both countries in this study: Italy and Australia. Children as young as three and four could recognize the distinction between a lie told knowingly and a mistaken false utterance by a speaker who intends to tell the truth.[6]

Research suggests that recognizing lying behavior may be linked to possessing the skill known as "theory of mind" which allows a child to interpret the mental state of another. Theory of mind is directly linked to developing moral character. Simon Baron-Cohen, in his book *Mindblindness*, explains that an individual can read the behaviors of others in terms of volitional mental states (desire and goal) and can read eye direction and predict some intention by this eye gaze. The research found that children with autism have difficulty recognizing facial expressions, following a person's eye gaze, and understanding what the person is thinking.[7] Steven Pinker, Massachusetts Institute of Technology professor and author of *The Language Instinct*, says that we can't really read other people's minds, but we can make "good guesses" by what they show on their faces.[8]

Successful communication is based on the ability to interpret others' mental states and develop trust and cooperation during interactions. Children who do not understand facial expressions or read their subtle cues may misperceive what the person is trying to say and act inappropriately in response. Their response will give the other person a signal that the speaker is not empathic and doesn't "get" what he wants him to understand. Some children need help interpreting facial and emotional reactions, as well as instructions on how to respond appropriately to moral transgressions.

Empathy and the Brain

There is considerable controversy regarding how emotional responses activate neural responses that relate to empathy. Researchers agree that when the brain responds to other people's emotions, there are three cognitive skills needed to acquire empathy: the ability to share another person's feelings, the ability to intuit what the person is feeling, and a socially beneficial intent to be compassionate to a person's distress.

One prominent view is that emotional responses are automatic and processed in the amygdala. This region in the brain has long been known to play a role in emotion and has been identified as the area where the most primitive flight-or-fight response occurs during stressful situations. When the brain is processing emotional reactions of others, this area will show immediate activity on functional magnetic resonance imaging (fMRI).

The area of social neuroscience research related to empathy is called *cognitive empathy* and links moral behavior with perspective taking, a process by which an individual represents the internal mental state of another and acts appropriately or inappropriately.[9] Similar to theory of mind, perspective taking involves associating a peer's distress with the action that caused the distress. This is what we call *moral socialization*.

Current brain research on theory of mind using fMRI has also shown that the medial prefrontal cortex, the temporoparietal junction, and the temporal poles are functioning when an individual is identifying the mental state of another.[10] When an individual is thinking about another person's ideas, his fMRI shows some changes to these areas. The evidence is not clear but it suggests that the brain is shifting when this perspective-taking event occurs.

Cognitive neuroscience research suggests that when an individual adopts perspective taking, the ability to understand the mental states of others, the neural circuits activated in the frontal cortex are the same ones used for executive function and inhibitory control. Executive functioning is also related to cognitive flexibility, which affects a person's ability to make inferences regarding other's mental states. The question they raise is whether perspective taking can induce empathic concern for those in distress and if this ability is motivated from a drive to actually help another person or to escape the situation. For example, when a child sees someone who is hurt, the child who is looking at the situation may have an immediate neurological response and feel empathy. But the child may also be fearful that he could be hurt by the same situation. The researchers found too that the ability to be empathic doesn't mean the child will act on his feelings and help another person. Being able to see another's perspective doesn't necessarily mean that the child will act for the good of others.

The mastery of perspective taking may allow children to look beyond themselves and learn to base their behavior on another's expectations. If preschoolers can learn to read social cues and understand the emotional state of others, they will be better able to socially connect and understand the moral rules of their culture. Our task is to help children develop a sense of moral understanding: to see how their actions affect their friends, be empathic to their friends, and recognize how they can be helpful to the larger group or even to the outside community.

CHILDREN WITH MORAL UNDERSTANDING KNOW WHEN THEIR ACTIONS AFFECT OTHERS

Successful children can understand when their actions will hurt another or when other positive actions will be good for the whole group. Teachers and parents need to seize on opportunities at home and at school when they can help a child see what a good action is and what a hurtful action is. Sometimes the best way to teach this lesson is with an oppositional approach.

Ann was working with a group of preschoolers on a hike near their school playground. Their teacher, Marilyn Walsh, was talking to two five-year-old boys about their relationship with each other. Her goal in this negotiation was to help them see how the boys could be friends, but they might hurt each other's feelings with negative comments. Marilyn suggests the opposite of the outcome she is looking for: she suggests separating the boys instead of keeping them together. The goal is to get the boys to see her "wrong" perspective and change their behavior on their own, without being told what to do.

MARILYN: Rowan, come here, buddy. You and Jody have always been such really wonderful friends. Look, he's already holding his hand out to you. Is that a nice thing, yes or no?

ROWAN: Yes.

MARILYN: Do you want to continue being friends, or should I lock him up over there and you over there?

ROWAN: Lock me up there, and lock him down here.

MARILYN: Okay. Off to the dungeon. Rowan did you hear me? What did I say? You could be friends and not . . .

ROWAN: . . . hurt each other.

MARILYN: Right. Friends don't hurt each other. But if you do, it's a mistake. If you do hurt each other by mistake, Jody, what do you do?

JODY: I go to the dungeon.

MARILYN: Okay. If you hurt your friend by mistake, what do you do?

JODY: Go to the dungeon. Oh, no! Now we can't play!

MARILYN: All right; that's settled. I don't have to solve any more problems. I hope that if you get a chance, you'll say good-bye to each other before you go to the dungeon.

Marilyn was using her sense of humor to describe what may be a good or a bad behavior within the context of a pretend story. She was trying to make the boys aware of how their behavior may hurt a friend. After her comment, both boys looked at each other with serious glances, put their hands over their eyes, and waved at each other.

Children will put their hands over their eyes when they are embarrassed and when they recognize that they said something that might not be appropriate. Despite the boy's uncomfortable exchange, they did learn to talk to each other about how they felt. Then Jody said, "Okay, it's not right. You don't have to come to a dungeon; you can come to my house and play." Jody was thinking about the consequences of hurting a friend and whether he really wanted his friend to leave.

On another occasion, Ann was playing with a group of three and four year olds who were in the blocks area of a classroom. Two boys, both serious builders, were building a huge ship and were talking back and forth about their plans. One of the boys introduced the idea of pirates who had been captured at sea. Ann was able to use the current news to help the boys understand how their violent words hurt each other.

Pirates are a popular story theme among preschoolers. Many have seen or heard about the popular *Pirates of the Caribbean* films. During this particular week, however, real pirates had captured a ship off the coast of Africa, and the story was all over the news. The class was preoccupied with the real story, and the boys were incorporating it into their play. They wanted to know if the pirates might come to the United States and capture them.

As she listened to their dialogue, Ann realized that this was a teachable moment—an opportunity to help them see beyond their game into the moral scope of their community and an opportunity to change their theme and the tone of their words to each other. Preschoolers need adults to translate their actions and help them make sure they understand what would happen in the real world. This helps children look at their own moral decisions.

ANN: Pirates are people. Do you think they could get better? Do you think they could be better people?

MICHAEL: Yes.

ANN: Well, maybe we could treat our prisoners a little better. How about food and water? They're going to die without food and water.

MICHAEL: Okay. How about if they get food and water and they can go to classes?

ANN: That's a good idea. At least you are thinking about how they might feel if they didn't have any food or water. (The boys continued to play on their pretend ship and capture more pirates.)

ANN: Where are you going now?

MICHAEL: To catch another robber, of course.

ANN: What are they going to do with him?

MICHAEL: Oh, go to jail.

ANN: Oh no! Throw him in jail! Aagh. The poor guy. Will he get to have food?

MICHAEL: No.

ANN: Water?

MICHAEL: No.

ANN: Oh.

MICHAEL: He's going to get a dry throat.

ANN: He's gonna cry and cry and cry in that jail, right?

MICHAEL: Yep. And he has nobody near.

ANN: That's not very nice.

As the pirate story continues, Ann encourages the boys to think about what they are doing to these pirates and what is correct behavior in the context of this narrative:

ANN: (The boys assigned Ann to the role of a captured pirate.) But I really want to have water. You've got to treat your prisoners nicely, right?

MICHAEL: Yeah, because we have to teach them.

ANN: Even robbers could learn, you know. I'd like a hot fudge sundae please. Can I have a hot fudge sundae in jail? But I won't take the whipped cream because I'm in jail, right?

MICHAEL: We don't got whipped cream.

ANN: Michael, what happens when somebody makes a mistake?

MICHAEL: They just don't do things right.

ANN: They don't do things right. Do you think they can learn to do things right?

MICHAEL: Yes, in jail, right?

ANN: But if you train them and let them out, they can. Right? They can get better, you think?

MICHAEL: Yeah. We train them not to be selfish anymore.

Young children know that they are in pretend play, but they also need to have the adults point out that if this happened in real life, prisoners would starve to death and die because of their moral decisions. They also need help talking about these choices. Some pirates will not change, but some will. The boys think about trying to give another person a chance and the consequences of their negative actions: tackling real moral decisions that they have created with their characters in play.

SKILLS FOR A SUCCESSFUL PRESCHOOLER

Here are some important big ideas we need to help children learn in order to master empathy.

Reading Facial Cues

Children need to observe and interpret facial expressions and emotional responses of their peers in order to develop empathy. And preschoolers need to be reminded when a friend may be scared or afraid and that they can help their friend even if they are fearful themselves.

Facial expression, body language, tone of voice, eye gaze, and gestures are some of the most difficult social skills to explain. In our experience, the best way to teach children how to read these cues is to point out how other peers are feeling in the moment. We've found that children learn to read physical cues from their peers faster than they do from looking at photographs or from direct teaching about emotions. Luckily with preschoolers, dramatic events are a daily occurrence. When they happen, help your child see the facial expressions of their peers and identify what was happening during play. Encourage your child to name the feeling associated with the peer's distress or the peer's response to an action.

Pointing out that Jimmy is in pain because he fell on the playground may give the child an opportunity to see his friend's facial expression and his body language. But this alone doesn't guarantee that your child will feel empathic toward his friend. He will need to see many of these same interactions with other children, across a wide variety of situations where a child shows anger, fear, sadness, disappointment, frustration, and other emotions. Stay at the child's eye level during play, and try to reflect the emotion of the peers. When appropriate, talk about how he feels if he can't express the emotions immediately.

You can also create a play theme with dolls or action figures and role-play with some characters that are feeling angry, sad, or another intense emotion. But the actual live interaction with a peer is the best situation to help a child feel the emotions of others and interpret subtle cues.

Avoiding the Negative Influence of Media

Many of the emotionally expressive images children see are part of our electronic world. Today's most appealing toys and television shows are not always on a parent's side of "right." Children are constantly exposed to violence in the media; and for some, it is part of everyday life. They need help making sense out of what they see, and more important, they need to be limited to viewing material that is harmful for their brain's development. The American Academy of Pediatrics has recommended that children younger than twenty-four months of age not be exposed to electronic stress, including television, computers, or visual electronic materials.[11]

When very young children learn from videos, they learn substantially less than when they learn from live instruction from parents and teachers or through playing with peers. Researchers found that background television has a disruptive influence on young children's language development and may cause what they call a "video deficit."[12] Background television consists of programming that is relevant but not distinctly designed to teach young children.

During play, children often reenact scenes that are violent or morally bad behavior. Parents and teachers can redirect this type of play to move a story from a violent theme to a more kind and caring theme.

In her book, *A Child's Work*, Vivian Paley sets the child up with information about the story before the game begins. She invites children to change roles and use language that leads their stories to a better ending—that includes their peers and does not encourage them to use violent words against each other. As an example, she suggests saying, "Okay, now I'm changing the story, and I want you to be the boy. Once there was boy who knew how to play blocks. He always let people build his own way. Everyone called him Good Player."[13] This is a strategy that parents can use to help children redirect story themes toward actions and ideas that are thoughtful toward others.

Being Aware of the Larger Worldview

Children need activities that direct their attention toward projects that help the world, such as protecting their environment. This idea is empowering and will help to develop their moral conscience as they direct their focus outward toward the whole world instead of just thinking about their own self-interests. This awareness helps build their own moral character and see that they are not the only person who is important. We have found that even preschoolers can understand how they can make a difference, even though they are small.

During preschool consultations, Ann met a teacher who was showing her students how they can help our environment and therefore the whole world. The teacher handed out a bucket filled with orange peels and compost. She selected three children to take the bucket to a compost pile on a hill behind the school. As they were hiking up the hill, Ann asked the three children if they knew what compost was.

One student announced with authority, "Well, you collect all the things you don't use after you eat them, and you put them in a big, mucky pile, and it's gross. Wait until you see it! Then you take it like fertilizer, and you put it in the garden and it feeds the soil . . . all these juices from my orange peel, and it goes down into the ground, and it grows flowers."

As they hiked through the trees, another girl suddenly dropped to the ground, pointed to a tiny green speck, and said, "Wow, that's near the compost pile. It's a tiny melon tree!" Her classmates joined her and examined the tiny green tree sprout. One child exclaimed, "Oh, we are saving the world! We really are. The earth will be better now."

This teacher was using a simple compost pile to help these children be aware of their effect on the earth, an easy lesson that you can use in your home as well. In this instance, the class knew that they were helping something much bigger than themselves.

Accepting Others Despite Their Differences

Preschoolers need help developing awareness that other children may be just as smart, or talented, or good at something even though they are in a particular group. For example, in some preschools, the boys call the girls "stupid" because they feel that girls can't run fast. They see themselves as "better" than the girls because they are boys and boys run fast and therefore are smarter than girls. In this next dialogue, Ann wants the boys to learn that the girls are just as fast as the boys. The purpose of this conversation was to help the boys become more aware of how they are generalizing or categorizing and how this categorization may lead to a division within a class community.

ANN: I have noticed that your dinosaur game involves all these really scary monsters, and all we girls get to do is huddle together and pretend we're scared. I like games where we can kind of be useful in the way we play. Because for the most part, it seems like all the boys are being scary monsters and the girls were being attacked by the dinosaurs, which seems like it's not quite fair.

PETER: As long as it's okay with them, we'll do it.

ANN: Well, I think that the better thing to do might be to say, "Who would like to play the dinosaur game?" or "Who would like to be a dinosaur with us?" This might be better instead of deciding what people should be. Maybe the girls would like to be the dinosaurs this time and chase the boys.

LILY: Yeah.

ANN: I think the girls should chase the boys this time.

PETER: No.

ANN: Why not? Shouldn't the girls chase the boys?

PETER: I don't want to.

ANN: I think it's fine. They can run just as fast.

PETER: I know.

ANN: You don't want them to because you don't think they should?

PETER: Um-hum.

ANN: How come? You don't think girls are good chasers?

PETER: No.

ANN: Why do you think boys should always chase girls?

PETER: Because it's fun.

ANN: And what do you think is fun for the girls?

PETER: It's not fun for the girls. It's not.

ANN: Maybe if it's not fun for the girls, maybe they'd like to chase the boys and have fun. Don't you think?

PETER: Um, no.

ANN: Don't you think girls should have as much fun as boys?

PETER: No girls chase the boys; the boys are stronger.

ANN: You think boys are stronger than girls?

PETER: Yes.

ANN: But they run just as fast as boys.

PETER: Well, I have my sister, and my sister is not as fast as me.

ANN: Well, some girls are really fast. Sometimes boys are stronger and faster, but there are some girls that are really fast.

ANN: Lily, do you think that the girls are as strong and fast as the boys, or you think the boys are stronger and faster?

LILY: Oh, I think they're equal, don't you?

ANN: I think they are pretty equal. The boys were thinking they are faster and stronger.

PETER: (growls)

At this point, the boys are still convinced that they are faster and stronger and have a right to have power over the girls. Ann's goal is to keep enforcing equality and the moral idea that girls are equal to boys. This will take time and patience.

TIPS FOR DEVELOPING A MORAL UNDERSTANDING

The following strategies will help parents and teachers identify what is moral behavior and discuss solving problems when there is conflict. These tips will help parents and teachers find ways to discuss negative emotions in play and ways to stay positive in peer play.

Share Your Home Culture with Your Child's Teachers and Friends

Parents and teachers can talk about cultural differences so that they can understand the moral and social values of home and school. Teachers can invite parents to come to school on special days and share their family culture with a lunch or activities that explain how their family understands language and moral values. Parents can also share with their child's teachers how they use language with each other in the home and how that can translate into the school environment.

Point Out Good Behavior or Socially Inappropriate Behavior

The parent-child relationship is crucial to helping a child understand what is right or what may be wrong in their behavior or the behavior of others. For example, if you want your children to be kind to others and to be aware of others' feelings, create a story where this does not occur and point out what's wrong and what happens as a result. When you show your child what could happen if she offends someone, the child may rethink what is happening and take more responsibility for her own statements and actions.

Use Real-World Events as an Opportunity to Teach Moral Issues

Although we do not suggest that you sit down in front of the evening news with your children every night, you can discuss with them, even at an early age, what is going on in the world and your perceptions of these events. Stories that make headlines are often moral issues. Point out the facts in the story and your interpretation of the underlying themes and how they relate to your family's moral code. You can ask your children what their reaction is and how they might handle the situation themselves.

Intervene in Children's Discussions When They Lead Toward Inequality

Provide discussions that will keep enforcing equality or pointing out that children of different races or religions are equal in intelligence or skill. Discussing sensitive issues such as equality in race or gender with young preschoolers will guide their decisions in elementary school years and beyond.

Teach Children How to Stay Positive and Avoid Negative Emotions in Play

Children who constantly talk about and engage in negative thoughts and emotions are more prone to violence and are less aware of the needs of others. Their moral compass is derailed. According to Richard Weissbourd, child psychologist at Harvard Graduate School of Education and author of *The Parents We Mean to Be*, "When negative feelings are constant and excessive, children are apt to develop primitive moral beliefs."[14] These children may feel unworthy or embarrassed, or may fear disapproval and isolation when parents use negative comments about their actions. This can lead children to lie, cheat, or commit other immoral acts in order to win parental approval. For example, young children may tell a story that is untrue in order to get their parents on their side ("I didn't lose my parka. Billy took it home."). Children need constant positive reinforcement for their actions and their accomplishments instead of negative ones from their parents.

Parents and teachers can encourage children to limit their negative thoughts and think more positively about their actions toward others. When your child uses negative words in play, make suggestions for more positive language. When the child's friend does something in play that is positive, praise the friend and repeat what he has done. If a child suddenly shares a toy or gives something up to your child, stop the play, and acknowledge this positive act. Reward the child by using positive affect and showing some excitement of this right way of treating others.

Praising children by saying they are "terrific" or "wonderful" doesn't help them as much as praising them for a specific action. For example, you might say, "I love the way you gave up that truck that you wanted and handed it to Mandy when she wanted it. That was thoughtful."

Teachers can create bulletin boards with positive words that help children think in positive ways. These can include photographs of children doing helpful things that make a difference outside their classroom, such as making a compost pile, collecting coats or cans of food for the homeless, or sending in funds to a project such as Greg Mortenson's Pennies for Peace for children in Afghanistan.[15]

In the next chapter, you'll learn how children use their moral understanding as they learn to become resilient to change and conflict. Children who can master the skill of understanding social, moral, and personal cues will be better able to deal with life when situations change for the better or for the worse.

IN SUMMARY

- Parents can create stories with characters that teach their children about moral ideas and how to treat others with respect.
- Children learn from their culture about family values.
- Parents and teachers can encourage children to limit their negative thoughts and think more positively about their actions toward others.
- Adults must point out situations in life that are morally right versus morally wrong according to the expectations of their culture.

CHAPTER SIX

The Importance of Being Resilient

PARENTS NEED TO FOSTER AND ENCOURAGE resilience in their children. Children who are resilient are resourceful and can adapt with flexibility to most situations, especially stressful ones. These children are able to regulate their impulses and emotions in order to meet the needs of a given situation, whether at school or at home. Children who lack this resiliency aren't flexible, can become easily disorganized, and often have low self-esteem. These traits are often the same as the ones that describe a "difficult" child who will have a much harder time managing elementary school and making friends. This chapter explains how resiliency occurs and how a child can develop coping skills to face situations that require resiliency.

According to child psychologist Emily Werner, resilient children are those who can overcome the odds against them and are determined not to let anyone crush their spirit. Werner studied children for thirty years and found that many were resilient and successful in school despite having a troubled or impoverished family life. She also found that resilient children had certain common temperamental characteristics: engaging social skills, strong relationships with parents, and the ability to build and tap into a community for support.[1] These children know when to ask others for help and are more likely to talk with their friends about their lives, which makes them better prepared for adversity.

RESILIENCY AND THE BRAIN

Why are some children resilient and some not? And what can parents and teachers do to help children become more resilient in everyday life, especially during a truly traumatic situation? The answer may lie in our DNA, our upbringing, or even in the brain.

The hormone cortisol is produced in the brain by the hypothalamic-pituitary-adrenocortical system as a response to stressful situations. This response system kicks in when a specific situation becomes unpredictable and uncontrollable. Children and adults who have difficulty in stressful situations produce more cortisol than others. For example, children who overreact to unfamiliar situations or people are known as temperamentally inhibited and don't bounce back and aren't resilient when a situation in life is traumatic or negative. According to Harvard psychologist Jerome Kagan, temperamentally inhibited children exhibit higher levels of cortisol than children who aren't temperamentally inhibited.[2]

Repeated exposure to high levels of cortisol has been found to have a negative effect on children's development.[3] These children have difficulty adapting to any situation that is unpredictable or stressful. And more important, they are less likely to develop good social connections with peers.

The way we interact with our young children has a strong impact on their ability to be resilient under stress, which will lower cortisol levels. Often parents choose one of two response models during a stressful situation: they respond with either effective guidance or negative interactions. Effective guidance happens when the parent has a positive orientation to the child and provides adequate structure and instruction. The child is compliant and responds positively back to the parent. For example, if a child breaks a dish, an effective guidance response would be, "I see you broke a dish. Now let's clean it up before anyone gets hurt."

A negative interaction occurs when there is parental intrusiveness or hostility. In the same situation, a negative interaction might provoke the following parental response: "I'm so angry that you broke the dish. You're so clumsy. I can't leave you alone for even one minute!"

Not surprisingly, negative parent-child interactions are associated with cortisol increases. What's more, recurring negative parent-child interactions elicited significantly stronger cortisol reactions each time. However, children who are thought to be resilient and were exposed to negative parent-child interactions are not usually affected by their parents' negativity. Yet children who are labeled as not resilient and were exposed to negative parent-child interactions showed significant increase in cortisol levels.

Repeated exposure to negative parent-child interactions that are intrusive or hostile should be avoided. Amy McCready, founder of Positive Parenting Solutions, stated in the *New York Times* that "screaming is the new spanking." She is referring to a growing parenting practice where frustrated parents who have learned not to spank feel that yelling at their child is acceptable and not harmful. Yet studies show that children are negatively affected. We believe that yelling should be avoided because it is at best ineffective and at worse damaging to a child's sense of well-being and self-esteem. "It isn't the yelling per se that's going to make a difference, it's how the yelling is interpreted," said Ronald P. Rohner, director of the Ronald and Nancy Rohner Center for the Study of Interpersonal Acceptance and Rejection at the University of Connecticut. As McCready says, if a parent's tone of voice is angry, insulting, or sarcastic, the child can perceive the message as a sign of rejection, creating a lasting sense of negative interaction between the parent and the child.[4]

If this is the case and the "quick response" reaction of parents is to scream, then we are raising a group of youngsters who won't be resilient because they lack self-esteem and a sense of well-being. They'll behave with others as they have been treated by their parents and others. Worse, their elevated cortisol level might become for them the new normal, and these children may need extra help to survive everyday events. These children will need support by professional family counselors and psychologists to help the entire family dynamic. Children who live in constant negative situations every day need help to reenter a life without this trauma. They will be hypervigilant, anxious, and nontrusting of other human beings. It will take time to help them trust others and to regain their own self-confidence in communication with others.

RESILIENCY AND EVERYDAY COPING SKILLS

Parents and teachers can help a child become more resilient by first building a clear and comforting relationship with her, so that the child feels safe and believes that she is part of a larger community. Knowing this, the child will feel more comfortable taking on new challenges because she knows that someone is looking out for her.

Once this bond is established, parents and teachers need to identify or create coping strategies for their children when they are faced with stressful situations. Preschoolers can become stressed by the most innocuous everyday challenges with their family, their friends at school, and even their own lives. When children are on a typical preschool playground, they run fast, talk fast, push, and sometimes shove each other. These actions and communications cause some children stress, particularly children who are shy, temperamentally inhibited, and not resilient.

Parents and teachers need to be observant and watch their child's face for any signs of stress or worry. As soon as children exhibit stress, adults can talk to the child, ask questions, investigate the problem, and make suggestions that can resolve the situation. This support will help a child realize that there is a community to depend on. Be sure to use a calm tone of voice when discussing scary topics that may increase your child's fear. When you get home, you can role-play specific situations in order to practice what your child should say when he is uncomfortable or afraid. With your help, the preschooler will eventually be able to develop a larger repertoire of appropriate responses to his peers and others who are causing stress.

Parents and teachers can set up rules, strategies, and even visual aids that set boundaries, explain uncomfortable situations, and even comfort a child in stressful situations. One five-year-old boy approached Ann in tears, saying, "I just can't get my snowsuit on, and my hat, and my boots, and my backpack and get in the car. Daddy is always angry because I'm not ready to go to school on time!"

Ann suggested that the parents set up a series of photographs by their back door where their son usually gets ready to leave the house. The photos created a step-by-step system that showed the boy putting on his sweater, then his snow pants, then his boots, then his parka, then his hat, and his mittens and finally his backpack. The last photo was of him marching out the door to see his dad smiling. Ann had the family practice the whole sequence of steps with the photos, and the preschooler learned to put on his outdoor gear without help. From that point on, he got ready for school, and he was happy. Best of all, the parents learned that even simple strategies like this one can help encourage that child to succeed and to feel more resilient when other challenges come along.

There is no template for ending stress. Parents need to be able to step back and reflect in the moment. Then they can see exactly what is or what has happened and find ways to change the whole situation for the child so that the next time something occurs, it is much less stressful.

Children Fear the Unknown

Even resilient preschoolers are often afraid of new people, new places, or new events. The most resilient ones will be able to visualize "new" as success: they have the innate ability to visualize a positive outcome in any situation. Others may want to know in advance what to expect: what a place is like, and if they get to take lunch, and if their parents can come to the excursion. They worry about everything before they get there.

Parents and teachers can preteach a new situation by explaining what to expect so that less resilient children can be prepared.

They must also listen to their children and ask them to verbalize their fears about the unknown. Once they understand why a child is fearful, they can address the specific fear and provide strategies to help the child accept the change.

Ann once visited a preschool located near an apple orchard. One preschooler told the teacher, "I'm afraid the apples will all fall down on me, and I will fall down when I pick one."

The teacher continued the conversation by asking the child, "Why do you think that might happen?"

He answered, "Well, when Pooh was climbing up the honey tree, all the bees came out of the hole and started to sting him, and he fell down off the tree!"

The teacher responded, "But we are looking for apples, not for honey. Apples won't sting you."

The child said, "Yeah. But apples are in big trees, just like honey. We might fall down off the tree while we are looking."

The teacher said, "Okay, let's figure out a way that you'll feel safe when you go up the ladder to pick an apple. If I stand near you on the ladder, will that help?"

The child smiled and answered, "Yep."

The teacher watched the child and then added, "We can find a buddy for you who can pick apples with you. That would be better. Right?"

The child answered with a grin, "Yes!"

During the apple-picking trip, this child was helpful to others and even picked up a fallen basket that another child dropped. He was self-confident that day and was the first child to volunteer to share his thoughts with the entire class about his first trip to pick apples.

Resilient Children Create Options

Young preschoolers who are resilient are able to identify the different ways they self-soothe: what they do or what they need when they're worried or face a challenge. They may love to hug their stuffed animals, or tell their parents or their teachers that something is bothering them. Once they can talk about their fears, they may find new ways to self-soothe and figure out how they can bounce back more easily when things don't work out. The worrying then becomes a separate problem that they want to solve. The worries don't consume them and take over their feelings until they become almost incapable of deciding what to do next. This talking and problem solving with others is one way children who are resilient can return to play easily.

Ann was visiting a class of five year olds, and the teacher, Marilyn, was reading *Wemberly Worried*, by Kevin Henkes, a story about a mouse that worried. In the story, Wemberly worried like this: "What if the teacher is mean? What if I can't find the bathroom? What if I can't make a friend?" In response, the children shared their own coping strategies:[5]

MARILYN: I wonder if when you're feeling worried or scared, is there anything you do to make yourself feel better or less worried or less scared?

ANDREA: My mom gives me hot chocolate.

MARILYN: So your mom gives you something to feel better. Can anybody think of something that they could do to help them feel not so worried?

RICKY: I rub Lambie's ears.

MARILYN: So you have a stuffed animal you hold on to and rub? Anybody else?

TORY: I carry my horse.

MARILYN: So you carry something that you can hug.

ANN: Does anybody think of pictures in their mind of a happy thing that makes them feel better?

TORY: I think of me in the arms of my grandma and my grandpa in Florida.

HANK: I just hug my bear.

ANN: Do you ever think about talking about it to a friend or your mom?

TORY: My mommy comes to me and comforts me.

HANK: I just hug my bear.

ANDREA: I read my book.

RICKY: I play with my toys.

SYDNEY: I go skating.

ANN: What do you do if you accidentally fall and slip when you're skating?

SYDNEY: You turn over, put one hand on your knee (gets down on her knee and shows me how), and you get back up! (She demonstrates.)

ANN: What do you think when this happens to you?

SYDNEY: I get up, and I just keep skating.

Resilient children as young as five years old can explain how they cope with worry and stress and bounce back when things don't work out. This group of five year olds provided several strategies for coping with stress and worry and ways of getting back on their feet when everyday life presents challenges. However, sometimes life brings trauma to children and stressful situations that are unimaginable and uncontrollable.

RESILIENCE AND TRAUMATIC SITUATIONS

Some children can endure major trauma from war and yet avoid the negative impact on their well-being and emotional stability. Yaniv, one of our international patients, lives with his family in Haifa, Israel, and has survived bombings and ongoing violence. During one visit when he was five years old, Yaniv's mother explained that they had recently lost friends and that their family had been living with bombings in Haifa for weeks.[6] When Ann asked Yaniv's mother how her family kept their resilience and withstood the emotional impact of the bombings, she answered, "We always try to play a game with the kids of finding something positive in a given scenario. For example, the first night when we were all in the bomb shelter and the kids where quite frightened, we brought in a computer and a DVD; we all cuddled up in sleeping bags on the floor and watched a movie together. We made a big deal out of the fact that we have never actually done that before—just all cuddle up and watch a movie together—so there are positive aspects to being forced to sleep in the shelter."

Yaniv had a distinct way of dealing with his nation's crisis: he constantly repeated the sounds of the bombings and the way he felt about the buildings being destroyed. While Yaniv was living in Haifa, Israel, his home was close to many explosions from bombings during the war. He could hear the bombs as the family lived in their basement and dealt with the stress of being in a war area.

His parents had to cope in several ways with their wartime situation. His father said, "The best way to deal with things like that is by doing, by looking forward, focusing on what needs to be done, and where we can go from here, rather than becoming paralyzed because of what has happened. It doesn't mean that there's never time of difficulty and that feelings are being ignored, but I always see that the direction needs to be forward and not backward. If you keep that in mind, if you understand that you have responsibility, that it is up to you and it is in your hands to deal with the situation, and not just sit passively, I believe you can deal more effectively with situations and move forward much more quickly."

Two years later, Yaniv's parents once again brought him to see Ann just after another bombing. When Yaniv, now seven years old, walked into the office, he immediately announced that he might lose his house in Haifa and told Ann that he needed to build a pretend house.

Ann and Yaniv spent every session throughout the summer building a complex three-story house out of cardboard, feathers, tissue paper, tubes of plastic, and tape. He made an intricate house with seven bedrooms, corridors to hide from bombs, and a basement to run to when a bomb hit, as well as a place for food storage in the basement. He made flowers out of brightly colored tissue paper and placed a clump of them in a handmade window box in front of each window. He looked at Ann as he finished the last window box of flowers and said, "The bombs always ruined our flowers."

Then he told Ann about how he survived the bombs. He was clear and thoughtful about his descriptions. He talked about how he couldn't go to school because the bombs destroyed his school.

When Ann asked Yaniv how he was doing with the bombings, he announced to her, "Ann, if you have a family, you make a house and then you plant flowers. If the bombs come, you just go to the basement for a few days. You stay with your family and listen to the bombs. If the bombs hit your school or your friends, you are very, very sad. When it is all over, you just plant flowers again."

At the end of the summer, he came to his last session with Ann, insisting on taking the "house" with him when he left for Israel. He folded it up and put it in his suitcase. Today Ann has a photograph of Yaniv leaving her office, still smiling as he waved goodbye to her, carrying his folded-up cardboard house.

HOW ADULTS CAN HELP

Parents and teachers must have tools for children who experience a crisis. When you play with your child, you can use creative art ideas such as building a fort out of wood, or constructing a cardboard house, or making a clay model, or using paint so they can express their fears. You may find that your child will try to make sense out of the experience by using words to describe the project instead of her own trauma. As the child plays, praise her for using language to describe what has happened. Then continue using the art supplies to paint, draw, and otherwise create objects that can represent something the child sees in her mind about the trauma.

Encourage your child to share the project with family and friends, giving her additional time to sort out emotions and express them. When a project is complete, allow the child to keep it where she can see it. These objects may trigger sad feelings and at the same time allow her to express her emotions to others.

We are constantly surprised by the way children learn to cope not only in everyday situations that are stressful, but in tragic circumstances of loss that are completely out of their control. Sometimes the best lessons come from peers who help classmates during a frightening time, like a fire drill, and say, "It's okay. The firemen are good guys. But you have me too. I'm scared with you."

Parents and teachers can help a preschooler who endures traumatic situations or loss by being present, being close, and listening to their pain. Ann treated ten preschool children who lost a parent or a sibling in the horrible crash of Flight 11 on September 11, 2001. The following description is taken directly from Ann's clinical notes on September 13, 2001:

> It is 10 AM on the playground [in Cambridge, Massachusetts] today, two days after Flight 11 crashed. The teachers are nervous, and the children are playing. The airports, bridges, and main roads are closed. I look up at the sky without a single plane flying above the city skyline. The sky is bright blue with white clouds that are in contrast to the horror of Ground Zero in New York. I walk through Harvard Yard and I enter another preschool. Several children are out on the play yard structures.
>
> One child after another tells me his story. I listen, feel, and grieve with them. I take their hands, I run with them, I slide with them, and I play with them, in silence. There is no talking. Our arms become wings, as we descend the slides and run across the play yard. I hear our feet as we run and pound the grass with each step. I watch one child as he runs fast with arms extended. He crashes into the slide structure and falls to the ground.
>
> "I died," he says as he picks himself up to run again. The normal sounds of children on a play yard are gone. There is only movement, sounds of feet running, and some chatter.
>
> A teacher sits on a wooden bench holding a child in her lap; another child is leaning against her leg. She looks up at me as I walk across the sand pit toward her bench. A young preschooler reaches up from the sand and throws a shovel at my shoe. I stop. He moves toward his teacher and climbs up into her lap.
>
> "Hi Jack. Are you saying hello?" I ask. He nods to me yes.
>
> "Use some words, Jack," I ask.
>
> "I'm scared," he says. "The planes will crash and get us."

"I know you must be afraid, but today is quiet. There are no planes in the sky today," I say. He looks up and then looks at me. We smile at the same time. I reach out my hand and he places his hand in mine. I bend down to watch his eyes.

"My dad is gone away. He is in heaven," he says.

"I'm sorry. I didn't know," I say.

"He is dead and he'll never come to my birthday party again," he says.

"That's so terrible," I say. "Do you need a hug?" I ask.

He answers, "No, thank you."

I pick up his red plastic shovel and hand it to him. He slowly climbs down from his teacher's lap. He walks to the sand area. He reaches out with his shovel and digs. He digs a deep hole, flipping sand up with each stroke. He stops and puts his hand in the hole as tears stream down his face. Tears fill my eyes. I can barely see his face as my tears blur my vision. He hands me the shovel. He sees my tears fall on his hand. I dig without flipping sand.

He watches me dig and says, "That's nice work, Ann. Let's build a new house."

When a sand structure falls over, I scoop up the sand and pat it back into place. Jack follows me. He picks up the second part of the structure and pats it into place. We are connected in our play and in thought. We move on. We pat and build and pat and build again.

There are times in therapy when I cannot use words; sometimes only gestures can soothe a child in pain. During the moments of silence I join the child in play. I play with an object that is similar to the child's toy. I pick up a shovel to join Jack. I kneel down in the sand, close to him. I am not too far away from him—close, but separate. I move slowly. I calculate my digging. I don't disrupt the sand. I keep my actions predictable. I watch his face and his movements. I stay with him and wait until he speaks. When he wants to build a new house, I know that we will move on to a new subject. I know he feels my presence because when I move my hand or the shovel, he watches and moves with me. When he moves, I move with him. With gesture and facial expression, I acknowledge his pain. I dig sand with him. He makes the suggestion of the next action in our story. I follow each move he makes. I watch his gesture, listen intensely to his tone of voice and I study his face.

Over many years I have learned that to be with a child in pain is to be quiet, pensive, and present. Each second counts. Each gesture means a lot to the child. Each comment connects to the thought of the child at that moment. Each play action or gesture brings us closer.

TIPS FOR BUILDING RESILIENCY

The following strategies will help adults find ways to be with a child in stress as well as ways to talk to children about feelings of fear and loss. We hope these tips will help a teacher or a parent lead a child toward more resiliency and less fear.

Never Make Fun of Your Child, Even If You Feel the Situation Is Justified

A less resilient child will respond negatively and cry if an adult teases her or makes the child feel less wanted or less competent. Children need to be told that they are wonderful, vibrant, and strong with great potential to be terrific in whatever they choose to do in life. They also need to be told with specific descriptions about what they are doing that is great.

If a child is willing to express his innermost fears, guide him in naming how he feels. Praise his efforts when he tries to talk about his emotions. Ask the child, "Are you scared?" Tell him that it's okay to be scared, and validate how he feels. Kneel down next to the child, and stay close to him. Suggest language that might be what he is feeling. If he imitates the language, he is probably feeling what you suggest. Once he says, "I'm so afraid!" you can say, "I know you are scared. It's okay to be scared. This is a scary place! Hey, it's great that you told me."

Share Stories About Fictional Characters Who Experience Worry, Fear, or Sadness or Are Clearly Brave in Adversity

Talk about the characters, and then ask your child what she is experiencing when she feels this way. For example, a wonderful photography picture book, *Stranger in the Woods*, by Carl Sams II and Jean Stoick, tells the story of a group of animals who are afraid of a snowman. The animals decide how they are going to approach this scary and unfamiliar situation with a "snowman person" in their woods. They each volunteer their ideas and show their fear and bravery. After reading, you and your child can act out the story, taking turns portraying each of the characters. By doing so, you are helping your child talk about the animals' fears as well as her own.

Another technique is to help your child set up play situations where she can work through her feelings about negative situations. Parents and teachers can encourage children to create story themes that reenact loss or fears. During play, talk about the experience, and join her by representing one of the characters. For example, some children are fearful during a fire drill, and teachers can set up a play scenario for a "pretend fire drill" with pretend firemen.

Describe Positive Aspects of a Negative Event

When children use words that are negative like, "I don't care," "I'm not good at that," or "I can't do it," try to find new words to suggest that there is room for improvement and that the child should not get stressed over failure. Encourage a child to use succinct, clear language that can express a sentiment like this: "I'm not great, but I can do it. I don't like this, but I'll try it. It might work!"

The next chapter explores how children develop flexibility and skills in compromising with peers and adapting to the needs of others in simple negotiations.

IN SUMMARY

- During a crisis, parents and teachers cannot ignore their child's feelings.
- Children can reenact loss or fears through play therapy and storytelling.
- Teachers and parents can help children create options to help them feel in control in stressful situations.

CHAPTER SEVEN

Encouraging Flexibility and the Art of Compromise

THE YOUNGEST PRESCHOOLERS FOCUS on their own world and struggle to understand what everyone else is thinking. They want to keep to their own agenda, hold on to their toys, and insist on doing things their way. They have strong emotional reactions to everything, even if they only gesture to explain their despair or happiness. By the age of three, children often refuse to do what their parents, teachers, or friends ask of them. And they learn that other people don't always appreciate their stubbornness.

The most successful preschoolers learn to bargain. A child who bargains is looking for a trade, or a defined agreement about what she can give to a friend or parent and what she will get in exchange. Children understand that if they agree to follow a request and ask for something in return, they may come out ahead.

Preschoolers bargain on the playground when they share toys ("Give me your front-loader, and I'll give you this tractor"), and they try to bargain with parents. For example, a child who wants to play a little longer rather than going to bed may say, "I'm not tired. I really want to play with this car some more. I'm building a car wash. I'll pick up real fast if you let me stay up a few more minutes."

His mother may respond, "Okay. If you agree to pick up fast, I'll give you ten more minutes to play."

Bargaining eventually leads to the acquisition of a more subtle skill: compromising. Successful children know how to choose their battles and how to focus on the best outcome. When such a child begins to compromise, she'll settle a dispute with another child by reaching an agreement where each side gives up her own plan and the two construct a new plan together. Unlike striking a bargain and sharing toys, children who are compromising know that they need to talk about the agreement and often give up something, accepting a standard that is lower than what they originally wanted. A good compromise occurs when both parties are happy with the new idea.

This chapter focuses on how children learn to negotiate and compromise.

FLEXIBILITY

As children learn to negotiate and compromise, they accept that they can't always get exactly what they want. This is a valuable life lesson: children who can look at a revised agenda or new situation in a positive light will be considered flexible to others and are easy to be around. Flexibility allows children to adjust to new places, new ideas, and new circumstances. Flexible children work well in groups and change the agenda of their play to accommodate others, which makes them fun to be with.

Not every child understands the benefits of flexibility. Many young children need to be taught that change is inevitable, and when it does happen, flexibility pays off. Young children need to see the ramifications of conflict: that even when they disagree with their parents, teachers, siblings, or peers, they can resolve their differences by reaching a compromise. Most important, they need to know that people who disagree can remain friends.

Flexibility is essential for the successful socialization of preschoolers. We know that children learn most of their negotiating skills by listening to others, even when the conflict isn't resolved. They imitate what is going on in their social environment, from their parents' dealings with their siblings and each other, as well as their teachers' ways of handling disparate personalities in the classroom. They practice the art of compromise in the powerful engagement of play with their friends. At the same time, parents and teachers must learn mediation strategies and then help children become more active compromisers. The first step is to recognize the socialization developmental milestones of a three year old, a four year old, and a five year old so that you can set realistic expectations for your own child's ability to be flexible.

Flexibility and Brain Development

The new behaviors that a child learns register in the frontal lobe, or *cerebral cortex*, of the brain. The cerebral cortex is also involved in expressive language and assigns meaning to the words we choose. In addition, it monitors what we are doing within our environment, including how we initiate activity in response to the environment and the judgments we make about what occurs in our daily lives, including our emotional responses.

As children learn new behaviors and become more flexible, new neuronal connections are made, increasing overall brain capacity. In this way, the brain map is reorganized, or redrawn, validating the idea of plasticity. Previously scientists were concerned with whether learning was based on nature or nurture, that is, whether biology or our environment defined behaviors and beliefs. Today we know that these two are not opposite theories but instead are intricately linked.

How Flexibility Develops in Play

Three year olds begin to show socialization with peers as they acquire the learned behavior of flexibility and when they can relate to others during play. Before this occurs, they can engage only in parallel play and pretend play. Once they begin to play with other children, they often enjoy role-playing and creating stories that relate to their life at home.

Three year olds are not experts at planning a story, but they do know how to let their objects and figures move into themes as they talk to each other about what they're doing. They provide dialogue for their characters, including the use of representational objects such as sticks or leaves that become, respectively, a pretend blanket or pretend wand. A flexible and successful three year old knows how to take the lead when she is acting out a story, as well as follow another child's leadership. The flexibility of children, both those who are shy and those who are assertive, is determined by their willingness to play with others and let others take some control.

By the age of four, preschoolers are learning to sequence their ideas and beginning to understand how to listen and follow another who leads the play. Many four year olds want other children to join their play, but they don't know how to include them in their story. They still need help in allowing others to join them, especially with constructing a story theme that includes more than two people.

By the time children are four and a half years old, they identify a shared interest with friends. Yet although they are more physically independent, they still require a general guided plan of what to do with a friend. They need an adult to suggest a plan and help them sequence their play, including establishing changes to their themes. Children need adults to be sensitive and make suggestions during play so they can express their own ideas and emotions.

By the end of the preschool years, a child should have developed several friends and may even have a best friend. A five year old can bargain and may show that he wants to compromise by giving others toys, agreeing to follow other leaders, and giving in when a friend wants him to do something that he doesn't really want to do. He feels safe in these friendships and will do anything to keep this relationship.

At the same time, five year olds want to be in charge, and they want an adult to be subtle and discrete with suggestions. The adult must become a member of the play, almost a friend, and take a role as one of the peers. As the play evolves, the adult can weave in the social skills and the language the child may need to interact. The five year old is beginning to learn how to see another child's perspective, and the adult can identify this for the child. This learning is critical to the child's later social and emotional development.

CHILDREN CAN MODEL ADULT NEGOTIATION SKILLS

Parents who master the art of negotiation and compromise are much more successful in transferring these skills to their children. According to Harvard law professors Roger Fisher and William Ury, best-selling authors of *Getting to Yes*, successful negotiation has distinct steps that help two people in a dispute reach good compromise.[1] The basic five steps are just as useful for children as they are for adults.

Step 1: Don't Bargain Over Position

Steer your child away from bargaining over how to be the "best" or the "fastest" or the "first" in line, in class or in events at school or at home. Ann was working with a four-year-old child who always wanted to be first in line. But as much as he insisted, his classmates never gave into this request. So the teacher set up a logical sequence of who would be the line leader each day of the week. When Jimmy continued to complain, his classmates had the tools to say, "You know you can't be the line leader every day!"

The second aspect of this rule is that during a negotiation, each child must let go of the need to save face or place blame. Fisher asks that all parties put themselves in the shoes of the other people in order to find out what they are thinking or feeling. For example, if a parent wants a child to clean up his room, they must begin the negotiation with a request instead of finding fault. If a parent tells a child, "Your room is always a big mess!" the parent is blaming, not negotiating, and thus creating an emotional attack. Instead, the parent should ask the child why he is not cleaning up his room. It could be that the child is too tired from a long day at school, or thinks that the task is too daunting and quits, or is having so much fun playing that that he doesn't want to stop. And maybe the reason is that cleaning his room is boring.

Step 2: Separate the Emotional Dispute and the People from the Actual Problem

Negotiations involve two people who have an emotional connection to winning their argument. These same people can also have different backgrounds, values, and viewpoints. In this step, everyone involved is allowed to share their cultural differences as well as their diverse opinions. For example, children can take turns explaining how they resolve differences in their homes, and then have a chance to verbalize their understanding of the specific situation at hand.

Sometimes you may need to calm an emotional child by responding with a calm voice. Have the child take a few deep breaths, and then stay close to him. Explain that the problem is something that can be worked out and is separate from his hurt feelings. Defuse the situation by reviewing the problem in detail, and include both sides of the argument.

Ann used this technique when she was working with two five year olds who both wanted the same truck. One child said, "Oh, I never get the red truck!" The other child said, "Well, I want to be a fireman and I need the red truck." Ann explained that there was only one red truck and asked the boys to think of some solutions for this problem. She engaged the boys in explaining their own positions, and they began to talk about the "problem" as something "between" them and not just a problem for one person. The problem became a separate subject. Soon one child announced, "Okay, you can have the red truck for a little while, but I want it after you're done being a fireman."

Step 3: Focus on Achieving a Shared Interest

Just like adults, children are capable of understanding that there are two sides to a disagreement. But in order to resolve a dispute, they need to understand the underlying issue that motivates each person. The helpful parent can rephrase what each child believes in a positive way so that neither side is "at fault." In this way, they will be able to uncover what Fisher refers to as a "shared interest." A common shared interest for preschool-age children is the need to be social, or to please others, including their friends, parents, and other adults around them.

Once, while working with two quarreling four year olds, Ann asked the girls, "What is the most important thing? Do you want to stay friends forever?" They answered, "Yep!" Their shared interest was that they both wanted to remain friends. That knowledge helped end the quarrel.

Step 4: Invent and Create Options for Mutual Gain

Rarely is there a single right answer for adults or children during a negotiation. Instead of rushing to end an argument between quarreling preschoolers, brainstorm options with them to solve the problem so that each child feels that the compromise they reached is a good one.

A negotiation has no single right answer for either adults or children. That means an adult should not rush to end an argument for quarreling toddlers by imposing a solution on them. Instead, brainstorm options with them so that each child can own part of a potential compromise. Identify the interest they share in their play. Once the discussion is finished, make a list of the most promising ideas.

Step 5: Insist on Using Objective Criteria

Young children are most sensitive to perceptions of fairness. They want others to agree on what the basic rules or criteria should be in any negotiation. You can help your child create a list of ideas that outline what is considered fair in any particular situation. Then when they are in the heat of an argument or negotiation, they can have a frame of reference to use in deciding the best way to reach a resolution or compromise. The children can use their rules to talk about their differences and take turns presenting their ideas. This also allows children to talk through their issue instead of pressuring each other with threats or a simple refusal to budge.

Taking a step back from an argument also allows the adult an opportunity to review the ground rules for reaching a compromise. One rule may be that no child is allowed to be physical during a negotiation: no hitting, biting, or kicking. Another rule can be that children are not allowed to say mean things or retreat from the discussion until it is settled.

THE BENEFIT OF ADULT INTERVENTION

In order to be successful at compromising, preschoolers need to practice with adult guidance at first and then try the process out on their own with an adult ready to help if necessary. In the past, experts recommended that parents refrain from intervening when children fight, based on the idea that parental intervention deprives children of the opportunity to learn how to resolve conflict on their own. Today this theory has been completely reversed: parents are now considered to be important in reducing conflict between children.

Children who are assisted by the parents during an argument will more likely give up their power-assertion strategies (taking over the play, grabbing toys, or fighting) or retreat from play altogether, and they will instead start to negotiate and compromise. This will lead to an agreement in the short term and friendship in the long term.

Children whose parents guide them in negotiation are more likely to talk calmly, share perspectives, listen, explain, apologize, and suggest solutions than children who have not had have parental guidance. Children whose parents were trained in mediating conflict used more constructive conflict resolution strategies, compromised more often and had less negativity when they negotiated, had a better understanding of their siblings' perspectives, and controlled the outcomes of conflict more frequently than children with parents who had no training.[2]

Parents and teachers can set up and enforce negotiating ground rules such as these for their children during a conflict:

- Introduce the ground rules that reduce hostility.
- Identify the exact conflict issues and allow the children to discuss the disagreement.
- Foster mutual understanding and build empathy.
- Help children propose, assess, and adopt resolutions where all parties are satisfied with the new resolution.

Another useful negotiation technique is *scaffolding*, which we discussed in Chapter Four. With parent or teacher support and guidance in natural interactions during play, children can practice and develop this method with peers.

Conflict or the escalation to conflict happens in almost all peer relationships. Children can fight about anything, from toys, to clothes, to ideas. Through parent facilitation and guidance, they can learn how to resolve conflict and develop perspective-taking skills that will help them later in school. Some negative play situations can be mediated quickly, and others take time. Sometimes in the heat of a conflict, children need to calm down and take a time-out. Then the negotiation strategies can be more helpful. It may take several conversations with adult support before children can resolve their issues and agree on something new.

Ann was working with two five year olds who were playing in the block corner of their preschool class. They were constructing together and negotiating over what to build, where to build the structures, and how to include the characters: some dolls and a big dinosaur.

JUDITH: Pretend this is the daddy, and pretend this is the mommy, and these are the two kids.

ANN: So what's this part of the house?

JUDITH: This is the roof, and this is the door.

AARON: This dino eats houses! (Aaron moves his arms in a threatening way toward the other child and uses a loud, angry voice.)

ANN: Oh, my goodness! (Ann wants to protect the other child and uses a concerned facial expression and moves close to both children in the block area.)

In this situation, some parents or teachers might tell Aaron that he should stop making his dinosaur eat the house and that his dinosaur is too "mean," or they may change the dinosaur into another object entirely, such as a car or a spaceship. But in the end, the disheartened child will leave the play area. Both children are left without a playmate and are unhappy.

Instead, Ann guided the story theme and made concrete changes to help Aaron continue to play with Judith and also to give up his control of his angry dinosaur:

ANN: The people have to go inside the house, but the dinosaur's gonna eat the people. What are you going to do, Judith? (Aaron is smiling, watching Judith.)

JUDITH: Well, the house has to run away!

ANN: The house will have to run away! You're right!

JUDITH: It doesn't have to stay there!

AARON: It can't! It doesn't have feet!

ANN: So, we're gonna have to make her house run away in case the dinosaur comes. Right?

AARON: He's sticking his tongue out, and then he's gonna eat the house up! (Aaron winds up his arm and makes the pretend dino tongue.)

JUDITH: Oh, no!

ANN: Oh, no, save your house, Judith!

AARON: It can't run away!

JUDITH: (Judith begins to negotiate to solve the problem.) You can have these blocks! (Aaron is lifting up her house.) Stop! I need my house!!! (Aaron places the house back down on the floor.)

ANN: Aaron, Judith wants her house back. That was good.

AARON: He only ate . . . you only have the roof now. (Aaron picks up the roof block.)

ANN: Oh, she has the whole house now. Did you save your whole house?

JUDITH: I did!

AARON: Okay, let's build another house for my dino.

Because Aaron was flexible, he was able to respond to the change in the story. Neither child felt that he or she had lost control over the whole story. Better still, both believed that they had created the ending and continued to enjoy playing together.

FLEXIBILITY AND CHANGE

One consistent pattern of preschool-age play is that children often repeat one story idea over and over again. The theme may involve princesses, a fireman saving a burning building, a spaceship, or Star Wars figures with light sabers, or they may mimic something they have seen in a movie or a character in a book. Sometimes children take ownership of one story theme, which leaves out potential friends who might want to play with them but don't know the rules of the game. Listening to a child who is stuck with one theme, such as Disney princesses, creates boredom for others, and eventually her friends will leave her alone and find something—or someone—else to play with.

When children are comfortable moving to a variation on the main story, they become more flexible. The adult's task is to teach the child how to be flexible within the existing story so that it opens the door for other children to join in. Suggesting new themes and ideas during play can motivate a child to develop his own thoughts and allow a new story theme to evolve through collaboration with an adult or friends. The result is that playmates share leadership of the story and become likable to each other. In this way, no one controls the agenda of play.

Parents can assist play in several creative ways as the child develops play skills between ages three and five. The differences are subtle but significant. Parents need to encourage the children who are playing near each other to remain physically close to each other so that they can interact. Three year olds sometimes run away from a friend, unaware that they are not paying attention to him or her. Three year olds also need verbal and physical gestures or cues from adults: facial expressions that they can see, exaggerated gestures, and voice intonation patterns that vary and show affect to the child. Three and four year olds respond to variations in the adult's voice tone. The three year old is not ready to see the perspective of another child but can learn to be sensitive to others and respond to other's emotions.

The following dialogue illustrates sisters who are playing and are locked in a particular story. Molly and Abigail are three-year-old twins playing with a dollhouse and figures in a bathtub. Both girls want their own dolls to stay in the bathtub. They splash water and hold their dolls in the small tub, but they aren't communicating their story. They begin to fight over who gets to hold the bathtub as they try to stuff both dolls in the tub. They scream and throw their dolls and the bathtub.

Typically in this situation, parents ask the children to disengage in their play since they feel that the interactions are not going well. They may remove the object that the children are playing with or put the bathtub out of reach. A typical three year old's response to this parent control could be crying or throwing toys. Instead, parents should direct the play in a different direction without removing any toys from the scene—perhaps varying the story theme in order to keep these children connected.

At this point, Ann takes a new doll, one separate from the dolls the girls are holding, and sets up a small swing set near the bathtub. Abigail brings the bathtub back, sits down, and watches. Ann turns the story theme from "the dollies that want to go in the bathtub that is too small" to "two dolls are going down a slide":

ANN: Maybe they'd want to swing or slide outside. (Ann sets up a swing set near the bathtub.) Oh, the ladder fell off. Here it is. (Abigail holds her doll and puts her back into a pretend bathtub, a small box.)

ANN: Here's Polly. (Ann takes another figure from the doll set and walks her toward Molly.) What's she gonna do?

MOLLY: Go on the slide! (Her other doll remains in the tub.)

ANN: (Abigail moves Polly into the box with the other doll and laughs.) Now what are they going to do?

MOLLY: Together! (She holds both dolls close to each other.)

ANN: They're going together. Look at this, Molly. (Ann motions for Abigail to move closer to the swing set.) They're gonna go on the swing set together. Watch this. (Ann gives one of the dolls that Molly is holding to Abigail.)

ABIGAIL: (Abigail takes the doll and puts it on the swing.) One on this! (The swing set falls over. Both girls are now looking at the swing set instead of the bathtub.)

It takes time to get the children interested in this change and learn the new actions with the dolls. They have left the idea of playing with the bathtub, the old story theme, and are focused on the slide, the new story. They are not fighting over who goes in the bathtub first. At the end, Molly is so happy that she squishes the two dolls together in her hands as if they were hugging each other. She is so delighted that the dolls are playing together! She is also thrilled that she is socially engaged with her sister. No one is paying attention to the bathtub that now sits, empty, next to the swing.

Learning to negotiate during the heat of the moment is difficult for young children, especially during play. But adults face the same obstacles, without the whining (we hope). Early one Saturday morning, Ann was driving to Harvard Square to her favorite coffee shop.

Brattle Street was lined with parked cars on both sides of the street, but she spotted a free parking spot and started to inch her way in. Then a driver in a small car challenged her. The negotiation began as both crept toward the spot. If they crashed into each other or into one of the nearby cars, the deal would be over. After weighing her options, Ann decided to give in and find another spot. After she parked her car, Ann walked down Brattle, and she noticed the same parking challenger walking toward her, smiling. Both entered the café and got in line for coffee. As she approached the register to order, her challenger glanced up at the cashier and said, "I'm paying for her."

TIPS FOR ENCOURAGING FLEXIBILITY

The following strategies and tips help teachers and parents teach the basic elements of how to negotiate in the play situation with a peer. The tips include ways to limit behavior and ways to use words to compromise.

Alter Your Child's Agenda During Play to Have the Experience of Another Person Making a Change to Her Story Theme

This will help your child learn how to handle change appropriately and possibly without a meltdown. Ann was working with two energetic five year olds during a play date. One child wanted to build a complicated car with interlocking plastic blocks and make his friend wait until he was finished. The second friend had already finished his car and wanted to have a car race. Both boys were about to scream at each other when Ann suggested, "Okay, let's help Jimmy make his race car, but let's agree that in five minutes, we race with two cars and maybe

---

not the one Jimmy is making. Do you agree that you want to be friends?" The children agreed. Ann then said, "Okay, then lets agree that we change what we are doing now."

Stop Play When Children Use Rough or Threatening Gestures

Help your child understand the rules of kind behavior and the consequences of negative behavior. For example, when one child hits another child, an adult needs to intervene. Once the situation is calm, the parent can ask each child to explain what happened, how they disagreed, and what the problem was that started the conflict. Then the parent must explain the ground rules of play: no hitting, pushing, shoving, spitting, using mean words, throwing things, or disengaging and running out of the play area. If the behavior continues, the children must not be allowed to play together until they can be empathic and kind to each other.

Support Compromise with Language Suggestions That Limit Peers

Give children the language they need to limit their peers when they feel they might physically collide with their classmates on play structures or in general play. Many children need help with what to say to a friend who gets too close or who encroaches on a child's play area quickly. If the child doesn't use language immediately to tell his friend to move over or give him room, he may scream, shove, and retreat to another play area. If the child is at school, teachers can make suggestions in the middle of interactions when children are too close to each other or when they predict that there will be a collision. An acceptable phrase to use is "Don't get too close!" or "Look out!"

With appropriate adult mediation strategies and practice, children can become more flexible and learn to accept compromise. When they master these new skills and develop new ideas, they will be happier and better adjusted emotionally. Their flexibility will carry over into other arenas besides play: they will be able to adjust to new situations, new people, and new places more easily.

As children mature, they will be faced with the challenges of using negotiation and compromise along with other executive function strategies to manage their play with other children, as described in the next chapter.

IN SUMMARY

- Children whose parents have guided them in negotiation are more likely to talk calmly, share perspectives, listen, explain, apologize, and suggest solutions than children who did not have parental guidance.
- In order to compromise, children need to grasp the shared interest in an outcome so that they can seek options.
- Preschoolers who can compromise become happy and more emotionally adjusted with their peers.

CHAPTER EIGHT

Getting Organized

IT'S 8:00 A.M. AS A YOUNG FAMILY prepares to leave for a trip to see the children's grandparents. The children have talked on the phone to their grandparents for hours in planning their upcoming visit. The grandparents are eagerly waiting for their grandchildren's arrival. The parents need to get their three children, ages two, three, and four, dressed and out the door with their backpacks containing their items for the trip by 9:00 A.M.

The parents think they're well organized for the tasks ahead, but the children are in total disarray. Angie, the two year old, is screaming that she can't find her pink socks that she needs to wear. Her brother, Billy, the four year old, yells at her, "They're in your toy box, stupid!" Jennifer, the three year old, is crying in her room because she can't find the special book that she made for her grandmother. Billy announces that he wants his Game Boy in his backpack so he can play during the long drive, but Dad says, "No! Video games are out. You need to be reading books." Billy and his dad are talking loudly as each tugs on the Game Boy. Dad wins, and Billy cries. Mom tries to do everything at once but is focused on Angie, who is still yelling about her socks, and Jennifer, who is tearing up her room trying to find her special book. Meanwhile, no one has noticed that the family's golden retriever is chewing up the lunches that were sitting on the bench near the door, ready to be placed into the children's backpacks. The floor is now strewn with torn lunch bags, carrot sticks, juice boxes, and a few remaining crumbs from the sandwiches.

We love this story because similar scenarios happen every day in every household. Our best-laid plans are often in disarray once our children are old enough to want things done their way. So how can any family become organized enough to walk out the door without creating havoc? Some days it's almost impossible.

We know how difficult it is for preschoolers and the rest of their families to be organized. However, we believe that preschoolers who can master the skills of organization can control their emotions, hold on to information, use language to express logical ideas, and execute their behavior to accomplish tasks, they will become a more successful preschooler.

Preschoolers are busy all the time, and by nature, they are disorganized. They need help from the beginning of the day until the end: getting dressed, eating breakfast, making the transition from one task or activity to another, and even going to bed. The fact is that preschoolers don't know how to organize a cubby, pack a backpack or lunch box, or get through a typical day, and the youngest ones shouldn't be expected to. They are still learning how to string together thoughts and formulate sentences that help them express ideas. It's a struggle for them to find the words they need to express their emotions. What's more, they have difficulty controlling their behavior, or switching from one activity that they are enjoying to another one, especially when parents or teachers ask them to do so.

Eventually, of course, most preschoolers learn how to be organized. Some master this skill faster than others, and the ones who do tend to be more successful. Our job then is to help them develop executive function: the skills needed to become organized so that they can follow directions, shift from one task to the next, make decisions, hold on to their ideas, solve problems, and achieve goals. Grasping these abilities makes them successful at home and at school.

MASTER EXECUTIVE FUNCTIONING

The term *executive function* is defined in different ways by different researchers, which can be confusing to both parents and teachers. Some define it as accessing working memory, while others see it as a combination of several types of organization skills. From a psychological point of view, executive function refers to a large umbrella of interrelated tasks responsible for achieving purposeful, goal-directed, problem-solving behavior. They enable both children and adults to override the more automatic thoughts and responses: they allow us to think through consequences and change our behavior to meet changing needs. Neuroscientists use the term *executive function* to mean a large umbrella of interrelated tasks responsible for purposeful, problem-solving behavior.[1]

These experts explain that executive function skills are adaptive, meaning that these skills allow the child to override more automatic responses and thoughts in order to move toward a directed goal. As the definition implies, these functions are particularly critical for problem solving: all of the skills that are connected and defined as executive function are the ones that teach children how to be flexible enough to shift from one thought to another or from one task to another. They help us become emotionally regulated enough to control behavior and organized in thought so that we can use logical reasoning and solve problems.

Executive Function and Working Memory

The first component of executive function is the development of working memory. A child who has good working memory can hold on to an idea, manipulate that idea, and make a clear decision.

A child with good working memory remembers that when she sees that it's raining, she needs to wear a hood or a hat and can visualize where a rain jacket with a hood is in her closet. She can sort out all the other items in her room, usually on the closet floor or in her closet, and immediately find that jacket. The child who has difficulty with working memory has a short attention span. She may remember only one step of a two-step direction, which makes it hard for her to complete any task, even one that she might enjoy. This child may have difficulty finding her clothes and books and may not be able to figure out where she is supposed to be. She may not be able to stay on one topic while talking to her friends and has difficulty retelling the events of an activity.

Another skill is called *set shifting*, which is a part of working memory.[2] The key aspect of set shifting is the ability to make a transition from one activity to the next, switch attention from the teacher to playing with a friend, or change focus and shift from one task to another. This skill is important in order to master problem solving or simply moving around a classroom and playing and talking to the other children. In order to do this, the child must first create a mental representation of a task, remember it, shift attention to the new task, and change from the old idea to the new one.

Problems with set shifting appear when a child doesn't want to leave the first task and go to the new one. A child who can't shift tasks can become upset by new situations. She will also have trouble adjusting to new people, such as a babysitter or a substitute teacher, which can leave her feeling confused and often vulnerable.

Executive Function and Emotions

Executive function also encompasses the ability to modulate emotions and emotional responses. Children who have difficulty set shifting likely also have difficulty controlling their emotions, because their confusion affects their ability to modulate emotions in any situation.

A child who has difficulties in this domain may be unaware of how his behavior affects others. He will frequently lose control and can't regulate his response to situations. He may cry easily, laugh hysterically when incidental things happen, or have a temper tantrum. He may act like a wild child or be sillier than his peers. He is impulsive and restless, and he often gets out of control and sidetracked during activities. A child with poor emotional control overreacts to small problems and has angry outbursts and mood changes. He can't see the big picture, gets stuck on details, and may be overwhelmed by them.

Executive Function and Planning or Organizing

The skills related to planning and organization are also part of executive function. These skills allow a child to manage current and future tasks within a situation. The planning component relates to the child's ability to anticipate what is coming next.

The organization component relates to the child's ability to bring order to his actions or collect materials or select things that will bring order to a situation. Children with organizational issues often approach a situation in a haphazard fashion and sometimes may begin by throwing things instead of selecting items or tasks. These children's bedrooms may be strewn with toys and clothes. One parent told Ann that she wanted to say goodnight to her son and tried to reach his bed, but tripped over his toys and then slipped on a jacket on the floor and broke her ankle in the process.

A child who has difficulty planning and organizing may try to put away big toys in small spaces where they don't fit. Or in the middle of that task, he may forget what he is doing and wander away. He has trouble thinking of ways to solve problems. He leaves a huge mess for others to clean up. As in the example of the three children preparing for a family trip, one child can't find her socks, another can't find a special book, and the parents are not planning the steps for their children to be able to get out the door smoothly. This doesn't mean that they all have executive function difficulties; it shows only that most preschoolers need consistent help with organization and planning skills.

Additional skills that fall into the executive function umbrella are described as *cognitive control functions*. This term can be used interchangeably with what we think of as organizational skills.

How Executive Function Helps

Executive function skills help children in a number of ways:

- Hold information in their mind.
- Shift from one task to another.
- Carry out multistep activities.
- Solve problems and make decisions.
- Control their emotions.
- Plan for the future, both short term and long term.
- Organize their materials for an event.
- Decide what to pay attention to in a busy sensorial field.
- Decide which activities to pursue and when.
- Organize their bedroom.

A child with executive function deficits doesn't lack all of these skills. She may be good at controlling her emotions but struggle to plan and organize. Or her working memory may be fine, but she is distracted when she has to change tasks.

PLANNING, ORGANIZATION, AND THE BRAIN

Executive function skills are connected to the prefrontal cortex, which typically matures later than other areas of the brain. The most important function of the prefrontal cortex is in regulating perception, thought, and behavior. Research suggests that the core components of executive function are present during preschool: working memory, inhibition, and cognitive flexibility (set shifting). However, each of these develops independently and at different rates.

The development of executive function skills is also related to mastering attention: the ability to focus on a task and ignore extraneous or irrelevant information. This is a necessary first step in any goal-directed behavior because this skill helps a child regulate activity in the primary sensory areas of the brain.[3] This means that a child can be selective with his attention and focus on the important aspects of what he needs to know to complete a task.

The primary ability to deal with conflict and overcome old behaviors, despite the pull of previous experience, is critical to the development of executive function during the preschool years. The most important period for the development of executive function is the first five years.[4]

DEVELOPING AND STRENGTHENING EXECUTIVE FUNCTION

You can help your preschool child develop effective executive functioning skills throughout the course of the day. You can help her plan her work or play, find materials she needs to get started, pay attention to her tasks, set goals, shift from one task to another, and cope with an unpredictable event. Parents automatically organize a young child when they take her hand before she crosses the street. Teachers organize class activities to fit the developmental level of the students and encourage the children to anticipate and become more aware of the next project.

Many preschoolers need their parents or teachers to preview what will happen next on trips and later review what has happened. Some children may need visuals to remind them about the descriptive language they could use to tell the story about an event. They may need to reinvent the scene and tell the story in their own words, but with candor and descriptive language.

On one trip to a duck pond, Ann worked with a teacher who laid out all the steps to explain what each child should expect during the planned outing. She told them that they would walk down the dirt road to the pond and put on life vests to keep them safe. She explained how they would be selected for rowboat rides and who would feed the ducks. Before the class left, the teacher showed photographs of previous trips to the duck pond and reviewed again the sequence of events.

The next day, the children were thrilled to see photographs of the new trip on the bulletin board. The teacher reviewed the trip again and praised the children for being in control and following the routine.

Organized Children Can Create Predictable Stories

Teachers and parents can create play situations that require children to practice sequencing ideas, including planning and predicting what comes next in play. This type of play between two or more children can help them trust their own social skills. They'll have more self-confidence when they face new situations and feel organized and know what to do.

Sometimes children organize their play automatically and know what to do. In this next example, Ann needs to make suggestions to keep the play organized and moving forward:

ANN: So, Simon, tell me what are you making here.

SIMON: I'm making a launching boat.

ANN: This is a launch boat, and what's this here?

SIMON: It's a slide for cars.

ANN: So is this going to be a ramp for cars? Is this part of yours, Simon?

CAMERON: It's for Roy's cars.

ANN: Oh, it's for Roy's cars. Barry, what are you making?

BARRY: I'm on the lobster boat too.

ANN: Is it part of Simon's boat?

BARRY: Yes.

SIMON: Actually I'm the captain.

ANN: Oh you are? How did you guys decide who was captain?

BARRY: We didn't. Actually we need two captains.

ANN: Oh, you're going to have two captains. Is that okay with you, Simon?

SIMON: Yeah. We need two captains.

ANN: That's great. So that's a paddle for the lobster boat?

SIMON: This is gas, right?

BARRY: Yeah.

SIMON: It's a gas paddle, right?

CAMERON: You have to get the paddle and get off the trap, right?

ANN: Oh, you guys have really made a plan. This is a very cool boat.

SIMON: Do you know what that's for, Ann?

ANN: What?

SIMON: A remote control that makes the boat go forward and backward.

ANN: Oh, that's really cool. You figured it out together, huh?

SIMON: Yep, we did. These could go forward.

Parents and teachers can reinforce positive planning when children plan together. The first step is to engage with your child and his friends while they play. If you compliment them on their work, the children will understand that their story or creation is important. Make clear statements directly to the children such as, "Oh, you really made a plan!" or, "You figured it out together!" which gives them the message that they are on track and working together through play.

It's equally important to name the objects they are building and use your emotional response to praise them for constructing together. They will continue their story theme if they receive positive feedback from an adult.

Organized Children Can Regulate Their Emotions

Disorganized children with poor working memory are likely to have problems regulating their emotions as well as their behavior. Adults need to help them recognize when they are becoming disorganized and then help their child get back on track. Even preschoolers can learn to monitor their own emotions.

Ann was working with two three year olds in a preschool classroom. Both girls were crying and wanted to take charge of the dolls in the house corner. They were pulling the dolls and throwing the clothes at each other, making angry faces and waving their arms. Ann suggested that they might want to have a birthday party for the dolls. Both girls immediately ran to the cabinet to search for the pretend birthday cake.

One child said, "I want to have the cake. I'm baking it!" The other screamed, "No! It's my cake!"

Ann worked with the girls to focus on their story, allowing them to express their emotions. One child told Ann, "Oh, I know I'm so angry, I can't bake anything!" The other child said, "Yep. We are mad!" They recognized the anger that was getting in the way of their actions in play and keeping them disorganized.

Ann then asked if each child could listen to the other's emotions and ideas. It worked. The girls told each other how they felt and then decided to negotiate over the roles. They agreed that they wanted to make a birthday party, but they had to be organized to do this task, and they had to control their emotions. By talking and listening to each other, both calmed down. Then they began to plan, and they eventually got to sing "Happy Birthday" to each other.

Organized Children Can Reason Logically

Children with organization problems often have difficulty using language. They may use the correct words but put them in the wrong order. Or they may need help searching for a better way to express their thoughts in a clear, logical way.

Children who have a hard time formulating a sentence can appear frustrated or even aggressive. A child who can't express his ideas by placing the right words in order in a sentence may push or shove or use some other physical gesture to get his point across. The other children can misperceive such gestures and start a physical fight.

Teachers and parents need to help frustrated children by rephrasing an incorrect sentence to make it clear and less complicated. If the child imitates the new sentence exactly as you said it, he is probably relieved and happy to have the words that express his emotions or ideas.

Successful Children Benefit from Organized Play Dates

It's not enough to just invite preschoolers and their parents to get together and then have the adults sit on a park bench or in the kitchen while the children entertain themselves. The most effective and successful play dates occur when the children are engaged with each other, not just in parallel play. In order to create an environment where children thrive during play, you must provide a plan that includes ways to keep the children organized and self-regulated.

Play dates are critical if you have chosen to home-school your preschooler. Not only will you have to organize the structure of her day, you will also be responsible for organizing her overall play, outside excursions, and work time. Make sure the day is filled with self-regulation activities, such as step-by-step outlines, lists, or schedules. Introduce difficult material as part of play dates and in small, sequential steps, using both auditory and visual tools. Keep routines simple, and repeat them throughout the day, especially during play.

To prepare for a play date, choose two or three activities in advance that the children will like. Once the friend arrives, clearly explain the activities to the children. It may help to prepare a physical list of these activities. Help the children shift tasks by showing them the list as you set up each new task.

You may need to play with the children to get them started. Keep the toys organized, and if too many objects distract them, remove some. You will know when there are too many toys around if the children are unable to stay on task.

A child who can't focus on a task during play or becomes frustrated when something changes in the play theme is demonstrating that he needs more parental support during play dates. When this happens, join your child to add structure and help him move through the steps of the play theme. Stay at his eye level, and repeat what he is saying so that it is clear that you understand the story theme. Then use simple language to rephrase what the children are saying and positively reinforce their efforts. This help will guide the play and keep the tasks within the play clear. The children will become calmer with structure, when they have clear tasks set up for them to accomplish. For example, one task could be to hold a particular action figure and move it toward another child's character.

Even for older preschoolers, play dates should last no more than two hours. At the end of the play date, provide your child with the words he needs to say goodbye. Later you can revisit your original checklist of activities with your child. Use it to go over what worked and what didn't so that he can check off his accomplishments on the original task list.

TIPS FOR STRENGTHENING EXECUTIVE FUNCTION

The following strategies are designed to set up situations to help children stay focused, sequence their ideas, switch tasks, and organize their day.

Provide Specific, Step-by-Step Instructions for Simple Tasks

Parents and teachers must be able to recognize when a situation is going to be confusing for a child and prepare her accordingly by breaking down each step of a task or event and providing clear and easy-to-follow visual cues. For example, birthday parties are often overwhelming for preschoolers. You can explain each step of a birthday party experience before your child attends the party so that she will know what to expect.

Visuals help children understand their current environment so that they can predict what will happen the next day. Something that seems as simple as talking about the weather can be confusing to preschoolers. The best preschool teachers use circle time to incorporate visuals at the child's eye level. The teacher announces who the "weather" person is for the day. Then the weather child looks outside through the sliding glass door to the classroom where she can see the sky. As the child is walking to the sliding door, the teacher explains that she needs to notice the sky and look for clouds. She holds up a visual of a cloud. She then holds up the rain, snow, and sun visuals and says, "I wonder which one will be the weather for today?"

Then the child comes over to the circle time area and joins her peers. She stands in front of the group and chooses the correct visual of rain, a cloud, the sun, or snow and puts the symbol on the board. The whole class then talks about what the weather is that day—for example, on a snowy day, what they do and what they wear. The child who has executive function problems is delighted with the whole routine and calms down. The next day of preschool is easy for him because he can predict what happens in circle time, and he can follow the routine. He feels part of the whole group and wants to be the weather child.

Engage Children in Physical Activity to Help Them Organize Their Thoughts

When a child is disorganized, take a break from the current activity: engage him in a game of catch, and talk to him as you throw a ball back and forth. This type of gross motor activity helps structure the child's thinking and keeps his language fluid and complex. It will also increase his ability to maintain a conversation, and he will even be able to have good eye contact as he talks to you. Once a child learns to engage in a simple physical activity, such as playing catch or shooting baskets, he will relax and enjoy the experience.

Ann was working with a child who was unable to organize his sentences. He switched topics, confused his word order, and often searched for words and hesitated when he tried to hold on to a conversation for more than two turns. Ann took him outside with a set of beanbags and some chalk to play a game. Together they drew a target on the sidewalk with the chalk and put numbers in the circles so that they could keep score. The game was simple: stand on a chalk line about six feet from the target, throw the beanbags into the target, and see who gets the higher score.

As they played, they talked back and forth. As the child became involved in the simple physical activity of drawing a target, throwing beanbags, and retrieving them, his speech became fluent, and he used clear and complex sentences. He showed no hesitation in his language. He was organized in his game strategies and loved the challenge of throwing at a target.

Switch Tasks Frequently for Practice

Children with executive function issues need extra time to practice routines. They also need more time when switching from one activity to another. A good way to practice both of these is to set up story themes that help children move forward and change to a new activity. For example, children in a preschool can practice leaving a play area and lining up to go to the library. Such changes can be difficult since some preschoolers think playtime is more fun than going to the library. But with practice, they will become more organized and take pride in changing with their class.

Assess Your Child's Emotional State and Plan Activities to Meet the Child's Needs for That Day

If your child is fidgety and complaining even before the day begins, try to find ways to engage him in some calming activity. He may need to get out some pent-up physical energy by running around the yard. Or he might need to calm down by sitting quietly and, say, looking at a book. Whatever your child needs, direct him toward a desired goal. You are helping him filter out irrelevant information from his environment so that he can direct all of his attention to a new task. Giving children what they need helps their ability to shift sets, or shift play, and will improve their ability to regulate their own emotions.

Next time when he is in this same emotional state, he may remember the activity that you suggested and do it on his own. The goal is to help children monitor their own emotional state and ask for or move into an activity that will help them regulate their behavior and control their emotions.

Children who are organized, can hold on to more than one idea at a time, and can regulate their emotions are ready to develop the leadership skills discussed in the next chapter.

IN SUMMARY

- Children's emotional state will affect their ability to be organized and to plan and make decisions.
- Executive function skills help children hold on to memories, organize thoughts, make decisions, and create logical stories in play.

CHAPTER NINE

Developing Leaders

ONE MORNING IN A PRESCHOOL where teachers encourage play and socialization, a teacher announced, "The preschool house corner is ready for the players! Look! The dolls are waiting! Oh, I think there's a dog in that family! Who wants to play?"

Three four year olds raced toward the house corner and scooped up their materials (dolls, aprons, cooking things, and hats), trying to decide who would be the "baby" and who would be the "mother," and who would be the "dog." No one wanted to be the dog.

Gradually one child stood out as the leader of the group. She looked at the two others and suggested, "Oh, say you're the mother. I can be the dog, because I know no one wants to be the dog. Right?"

Her friend announced, "Okay, I'm the mother, and you can be the dog."

The third child watched and listened.

The leading child added, "Good. You're the mother. Lucy, what do you want to be? Can you be the baby?" Lucy smiled and agreed to be the baby. Then the leader, Alison, announced, "Okay, you're the mother, you're the baby, and I'm the dog, but I'm a smart dog. I can talk. I can do more than just bark! Okay?"

At least one child in any play situation usually emerges as the leader: the child who guides the play themes to keep the story going.

Leaders are skilled at suggesting—not demanding—new ideas to the players and add greater detail to the play. They enhance make-believe while avoiding forceful or aggressive leadership. At the same time, a good leader is always scanning the others in the group and observing what is happening. She is organizing her thoughts about how to keep everyone happy without giving in to children who are aggressive. She has strong organizational skills and can assign roles to peers who will follow her because they respect her.

This chapter establishes the traits of a good leader, and how young children learn to lead with confidence and sustain positive interactions with peers without resorting to bullying.

Researchers have long recognized that children with leadership skills are more accepted by their peers than children who are demanding, whiny, and aggressive. A child who develops leadership skills in preschool is likely to experience more peer acceptance in the transition to kindergarten. Early childhood researchers who investigate leadership skills in young children define the ability to lead others as "play leadership."[1] This means that a child can be a follower as well as a leader and can act as a negotiator in play.

Good leaders can be followers as well as leaders and can act as negotiators in play. They know when to accept direction from others and follow them to complete a goal. They'll hold a tower of blocks for another child who is doing the building. They'll allow others to be first in line and not compete for the sake of winning. They are proud of their accomplishments and admire friends' accomplishments too.

Good leaders in preschool have self-confidence. They are fair-minded and show fair treatment to others. They can see the perspective of other children during play and adjust their behavior to accommodate their friends. They are also imaginative and create options when others disagree. They can lead simple negotiation. These competent children have the skills to create new themes in play and direct the play. Good leaders also have courage and accomplish their goals. A child who is building an airport out of interlocking blocks, for example, will encourage friends to help as he finishes to meet his goal.

Children who are leaders have mastered many of the other skills that allow them to be successful. Good leaders are often advanced learners who can use clear and appropriate language to talk with others. Preschool leaders have to be honest and inspiring to others. They can make compromises and engage in democratic forms of leadership. Leaders want the play to continue, so they look for suggestions that will keep everyone happy. In addition, children who lead others often accept positions in play that are not necessarily the dominant role in the story. They know how to use a friendly voice when they talk to the other children and give other players positive feedback.

Effective leaders do not give in to demanding peers and resist any child who tries to bully them. If they reject a peer, they usually can give a reason, or they can redirect the peer to another aspect of the play. For example, if a child wanted to be the father of the family in the story and the leader recognized that the child would be too demanding in this role, she may say, "Oh, this family is okay with just the mother. How about you be the neighbor? You can visit us? Okay?" If the child feels rejected, the leader may entice him into taking the assigned role by sweetening the deal. She might say, "But you're a good neighbor, and you can help us." The play leader is protecting her family of three and offering another role to the child who wants to be in the house corner. She is not saying, "No. We don't want to play with you!"

Typically good leaders are well liked because they have good communication skills. They are likely to use direct communication, retain eye contact, use a child's name, and move close to another child to talk. Leaders are also able to respond to others quickly and never ignore a child who talks to them. They don't say something that's irrelevant or demanding. Instead, they suggest an alternative way to play or another role for the child who feels left out. This keeps the talk between peers moving along and the story developing.

PRESCHOOL LEADERSHIP SKILLS
AND THE BRAIN

Research can confirm the brain's role in leadership behavior but cannot yet quantify how leadership occurs. What we do know is that the skills that derive from the frontal lobes of the brain, the seat of executive function, are key in creating the qualities of a leader. A good leader knows how to size up a situation, observe peers, and plan accordingly. These skills are identified through brain research as working memory.

Working memory is the part of the brain that stores information. It begins to develop around seven months of age when a baby can retain a representation of an object. By twelve months, a child can locate a toy that has been hidden several seconds before. A child who is a good leader needs to be able to hold ideas in memory and make decisions about how he is going to help his friends during play.

Torkel Klingberg's studies on children and working memory suggest that specific areas of the brain increase these skills during childhood: the parietal lobe, located just behind the frontal lobe; the upper part of the frontal lobe; and the anterior part of the frontal lobe.[2] Different areas are activated on functional magnetic resonance imaging depending on the task. Numerous studies show that the parietal and frontal lobes determine the child's working memory capacity. Since working memory is related to a child's ability to organize, his ability to lead others depends on this skill.

ORGANIZED PLAY FOSTERS
LEADERSHIP SKILLS

Parents and teachers can work with the leader child to expand a story or keep a story going during dramatic play. Adults can praise her for taking leadership and making suggestions to others. They can also be observant and help out when she is unable to resolve a conflict.

You can also make suggestions to encourage children to be empathic to each child's needs. Ann was once working with two children in the block area who were creating a pretend space shuttle. A third child entered the play area and announced that he was a fireman. If the leader decided to reject this third child's idea, the teacher could support him by saying, "Jamie, I don't think that Stevie understands why you don't want him to play a fireman. Can you tell him instead that you could all play in the spaceship and be astronauts?" The child who wants to lead may need some suggestions that don't reject the peer and give him other ways to participate in the story. Children do respond to and accept clear explanations when the story is changed or when the leader wants to keep the story the same.

Define the Role of a Leader in Play

Young children need to understand the meaning of the term *leader* in the context of their play. In one play session, Ann was talking with two four year olds who were moving large plastic dump trucks around the playground. They were negotiating, with Ann's help, about who was going to lead who and who would be first:

ANN: So you and Miles really took turns being the leader. That's really cool! What do you think makes a good leader?

ELI: Ahh . . .

ANN: What's a good leader? Somebody who knows how to lead?

ELI: Yeah.

MILES: Yeah.

ANN: What does that mean?

ELI: That's somebody that knows very good how to show people which way to go.

ANN: Yeah, that's a good leader. Is it someone that everybody likes?

ELI: Yeah.

ANN: And somebody that knows how to lead. What do they do? They think about other people, right?

ELI: They make other people follow them and they think of other people, right?

ANN: They think of other people and they help other people. People like to follow them, right?

ELI: Yeah. They help other people. Like when their dump truck falls over and gets stuck in a mud hole, they stop drivin' their own truck. They help the other person.

Compliment Children Who Recognize Leadership

Teachers and parents who give a child on-the-spot guidance during play can use their own language to help the play become more cohesive, that is, the story has a clear theme, including a sequence of actions by the players that makes sense to the children. The goal of language facilitation during play is to keep the children engaged and talking to each other. What's most important is to observe and recognize when they need help with who is going to lead the play. The leader in the play will take over, make the play more complex, and guide the others as they continue their stories.

First, your child has to recognize when he is being a good leader. Once he understands what a good leader does and allows another child to lead, compliment him. Find an opportunity during the play to point out to the children that they are being good leaders. These two boys were following each other by pushing dump trucks through the sand on the playground. One was in front of the other.

ANN: And you're a good leader, right?

ELI: Yeah. And Miles is a good leader too.

ANN: He sure is.

ELI: I'll go tell him.

ANN: You're going to go tell him.

ELI: You're a good leader, Miles!

MILES: Thank you.

ANN: You know that Eli said that a good leader is somebody people like to follow and somebody who thinks of other people.

ELI: Okay, Miles, follow me.

ANN: Eli wants to be the leader now. (Ann motions to the boys to switch places with their trucks.) Can you follow him? Okay, he's waiting for you. (The boys change places.) Isn't that nice?

ELI: Yeah. Thanks, Miles.

ANN: Now you're the leader for awhile.

ELI: We make good leaders, don't we?

ANN: You do!

Encourage Your Child to Be the Leader in Play

Sometimes children are reluctant to ask others if they can become the leader. When this happens, support the child in asking. Give him the language to ask, and rephrase it when he does use the words. Ask the other child to listen to him. Once your child becomes the leader, engage in the story and play with them. Continue to support the leader by complimenting the leader on his leadership role and have fun.

ANN: Okay, say, "I wanna be a leader now. Can I be in front?"

MILES: Can I be a leader?

ANN: Did you hear that, Eli? What'd ya say, Miles?

MILES: I wanna be the leader now.

ANN: Can he be the leader now?

ELI: Yeah. No problem.

ANN: Okay, there he is. He wants you to follow him. Now what are these trucks gonna do? Are they picking up some mud, Eli?

ELI: Yeah.

MILES: Ewwwuuu.

ANN: Oh, you've got mud! Wonderful mud. Do you like mud?

MILES: Yeah.

ANN: I do too. It's fun. You can make stuff out of it.

WHEN LEADERSHIP TURNS TO BULLYING

During play, particularly on the playground, children are literally thrown into an arena that seems tailor-made for testing others, creating confusion over rules of games, and challenging situations. In these situations, some children always want to control the play, be the leader, and take over the game so that they can be "in front" or "the best" or in some way "bigger" than their peers. When children create these types of intense conflicts, they are stepping over the line of leadership and beginning to bully. Psychologist Karin Frey and her colleagues coined the phrase "intentional aggressive process" when a child uses unequal power to cause harm for his own social benefit.[3] The aggression can be psychological, physical, or verbal.

The differences between being a leader and being a bully are clear. Children who are leaders are kind and considerate, use positive words to their peers, and never use verbal or physical aggression toward others. They stand out from the rest of the group and are followed and admired, unlike bullies, who stand out from peers because they are aggressive and want power over the group in a negative way.

If one child persists with verbal or physical aggressions against a peer or teases the other child in front of peers to gain control, he can create a negative reaction that can lead to serious conflict. Once bullying gets started, it doesn't go away. When this happens, parents and teachers need to intervene and help all children involved.

Types of Bullying Behavior

Peer disputes that lead to bullying behavior stem from two types of issues:

- Overt bullying, which occurs when one child wants power over another, which causes either negative verbal behavior (name-calling or teasing) or unwanted physical aggression. For example, a child may overtly disagree with a classmate and say, "You can't play with us, stupid."

- Indirect bullying, in which the bully purposefully manipulates the victim and tries to damage relationships with the other children. This child may say, "I won't be your friend anymore unless you let me use the Thomas Train Engine."[4]

Bullying behavior differs from the natural back-and-forth argument over toys during play. When two or more children want the same thing, whether it is a turn, or a toy, or a train track to go in a certain direction, or some adult attention, there will naturally be conflict of interests, but in this situation, one child isn't trying to control the other child totally. Sometimes peers bump into each other or crash into each other on a slide, and one peer becomes angry. These types of conflict are a natural part of play in preschool. They are not behaviors directed at intentionally hurting another child, either verbally or physically.

Not every conflict involves bullying behavior, but when a child hits, shoves, or pushes into another child's space in order to gain power over that child, creating strong unwanted physical contact, he has stepped over the line into a type of bullying. It is the intent to inflict harm on others that classifies the behavior as bullying.

When Bullying Begins

Bullying can become apparent in a preschool environment as early as the age of four. Researchers agree that school bullying is a widespread problem that compromises opportunities to learn. It is disruptive and causes social connections to collapse. Bullying causes class participation to decline, and children who are victims of bullying have poor academic performance later in primary grades and are less likely to attend school. Many tell their parents that they are sick and they can't go to school. Others refuse to go to school. According to researchers from the National Mental Health and Education Center Web site, children who are victims of bullying or bullies themselves show poor psychosocial adjustment and other negative behaviors.

Wendy Craig, professor at Queen's University and Debra Pepler, professor at York University, found that bullying occurs on the preschool playground, approximately every seven minutes, and is of short duration—thirty-eight seconds on average. The majority of bullying in their study happened within 120 feet of the school building. Boys bullied more than girls, but there were no gender differences in the type of aggression.[5]

Children who start to bully in preschool may continue this behavior and repeat it until they are stopped. However, when bullies are confronted with new ideas about how to build respect for their school and their peers at a young age, their behavior can be changed. Preschoolers can also become skilled at dealing with bullies, but they need help. A young preschooler cannot be expected to appropriately respond to a bully who is punching him or acting aggressively toward him in other ways. All preschoolers need to be trained to find an adult quickly and report the incident.

Parents and teachers can influence the seriousness of conflicts such as bullying between children indirectly by organizing time (giving the children structure within the play time, for example), space (allowing enough space for certain activities), and materials (giving the children toys that require cooperation with others) in play. Teachers can propose changes, set up rules to protect children from aggressive actions, and use verbal cues to remind children to follow the rules and be kind to their peers.

If these well-intended strategies do not work, the next best step is to coach children on how to deal with bullies. Luckily, some children can clearly express their frustration or anger. Ann once noticed a five-year-old preschooler who was verbally and physically pushed around by a particular peer. She was about to step in and give the child the right language to use in this situation, when the child announced to her, "He's a big bully. He needs you to stop him or smack him right this minute!"

How to Cope with Bullying

Some school systems have antibully programs that can help an entire community, and we recommend these programs. Nevertheless, on the playground, teachers need to watch children who are prone to this kind of interaction or want to control others in mean ways. The following example shows how an adult can reinforce what preschoolers should do when a bully confronts them, even though the talk occurred after the incident:

RUBY: Steven just stepped on me, and he put his hands on my neck. He's laughing.

TEACHER: Steven, go sit down. You can't put your hands on someone else's neck because that's very dangerous. When you breathe, all the air that you breathe has to go through your neck, so when you put your hands on someone's neck, it makes it so that person can't breathe. (turning to Ruby) So if Steven did something that you didn't like, you can come and tell me, okay? Because I don't want you to get hurt. But you can come and tell me.

RUBY: He punched me once.

TEACHER: What did he do?

RUBY: It was like, he like folded my neck really (pushed her head down).

TEACHER: When he does something like that, come and tell me.

Bullies Don't Always Listen

A teacher should always be present when a child tries to stand up to a peer who is aggressive. Safety is the first priority in these situations. Take the bully seriously when he threatens, and remove him from the play interaction.

In the next dialogue, the teacher tries to help a child talk to the bully who has punched her and needs help understanding that this behavior is not allowed. Although in this situation, the child who was bullying became calm and listened to the teacher, many bullies don't listen. This is why we recommend a schoolwide program that involves the whole administration, teachers, and students. In this case, the child did understand the consequences of playing without friends if he continued his negative behavior.

TEACHER: What could you say to Steven when he pulls on you?

RUBY: "I don't like that."

TEACHER: You could say, "Stop! I don't like that."

RUBY: I said, "I don't like that," and he still did it.

TEACHER: Well, then, that's when you walk away. You say, "No way!"

RUBY: And I walked away, except he keeps following me.

TEACHER: That's when you can come and find a teacher—if you've tried to problem-solve and it's not working.

RUBY: He pushed me a lot of times.

TEACHER: Well, maybe you and I need to go over to Steven and say that he's playing too rough. Do you want to come say that to him? (They walk over to Steven. The teacher stands close to Ruby.)

TEACHER: Ruby said she felt like you were playing too rough. She didn't like the way that you were punching her, and it hurt Ruby when you pulled off her jacket. Do you see her face?

STEVEN: Yeah.

TEACHER: Does she look happy? So how do you think you could do this differently?

STEVEN: Um, I can go? (He starts to leave the area.)

TEACHER: So how could we play that game without people getting hurt?

RUBY: Steven, come here and stop hurting people!

TEACHER: What can you do in the game so people don't get hurt?

STEVEN: Safe-play with them. (Steven comes back to the teacher and Ruby.)

TEACHER: You safe-play with your hands. Absolutely. Your friends were really kind of upset about the way you were putting your hands on Ruby's body. So you've got to think about that because they're not going to want to play with you.

STEVEN: Well, Ruby started it.

TEACHER: Well, you know if Ruby was doing it to you and you don't like it, then you need to tell her, and come tell me, but don't do it back to her. It's still not okay.

Parents and teachers must reward a child for standing up to a stronger peer who takes advantage of him. However, many children who are bullies do not respond to this type of interaction. Some educators suggest that the child use strong language or immediately say, "Stop! You're hurting my feelings by doing that!" Unfortunately bullies tend to continue to take advantage of the child and ignore the statement.

Learning Not to Bully

Later that same day, Steven became more careful around his classmates. He learned to keep his hands to himself and he was sharing. He had realized that he would have no friends if he tried to control everyone with his threats and abuse. Steven was listening to Ann's discussion with two of his classmates.

ANN: So he's a friend if he said "yes" when you want to play a game with him?

KYLE: Yeah.

ANN: So that's part of being a good friend, right?

KYLE: Yeah.

ANN: So what else makes a good friend?

ALEJANDRO: When you share. And you let him play games, and you're not mean.

ANN: To share. And when you play games. Do you mean let him lead the game, let him be in charge of the game? Is that being a good friend?

ALEJANDRO: Yeah.

ANN: What else helps you with your friendship? What do you think makes it work?

ALEJANDRO: Like when me and Kyle . . . we like to sit together and we like played patiently—[we] like both [waited] with each other to wait and go in line.

ANN: So you stayed patiently to wait with each other to go in line. That's a good friend, isn't it?

STEVEN: To not be first.

ANN: That's pretty good: instead of trying to be first, you let your friend be the leader.

This doesn't always happen on the playground or in school settings. Steven's change of behavior is an exception. Most bullies don't pay attention to conversation about how to be a good friend. They often have excuses about why they do what they do to control others. Sometimes a bully will blame the victim for his own behavior. For some reason, bullies think that they have some right to be mean. One way to diffuse a conflict between children is to talk about the event directly to them and discuss what it means to be a good friend with the other classmates.

When Ann discussed this concept with Steven's classmates, she made sure that Steven was close enough to hear the discussion. He could see and feel how his classmates responded without actually being in a heated fight. He realized that having a good friend might be a good idea.

Schoolwide Intervention to Stop Bullying

Schoolwide intervention to stop bullying is important. Studies have shown that comprehensive intervention can disrupt the increase in bullying. A program widely evaluated by schools as well as research is the Steps to Respect program developed by the Committee for Children, a nonprofit training institute formed after the school killings in Colorado at Columbine High School in 1999.[6] Participation in this program for two years was associated with declines in the rates of bullying and victimization.

This program insists on a schoolwide commitment to a respectful environment and that educators must convey a moral authority and be responsible when bullying occurs. This program also helps to change the bystander—the child who witnesses bullying behavior, who must send a message to the other children that he no longer admires a bully. Children who witness bullying must be taught that they are providing an audience for a bully and need to resist them by retreating and getting an adult involved.

TIPS FOR DEVELOPING LEADERSHIP SKILLS

The following strategies are to encourage teachers and parents to help children develop kind leadership skills, to stop negative behaviors, and to identify cues of the peers in bullying social situations.

Encourage Your Child to Listen and Observe His Peers

Bring children who are a variety of ages over to your house for play dates with your son or daughter. Sometimes children learn by leading young children. Set up play situations where your child is comfortable, and help him plan the play time. Always point out when his playmates need something that he didn't notice. Maybe one child wants to be the leader for awhile. Good leaders allow another child to be the leader too.

Identify Subtle Cues That Help Your Child See the Emotions of Peers

Children are often oblivious to others when they play. Sometimes it can seem that they are ignoring the obvious, especially if another child is crying right in front of them. Children who are well liked as leaders can read the subtle cues of their peers, including facial expressions and voice patterns.

Regularly point out another child's facial expression and voice tone, and tell your child that he needs to notice these cues so he can see how the other feels. Children need to be taught how to read and interpret others' subtle language (voice tone and volume), gesture, body cues, and facial expressions.

Be Mindful of Bullying and How Your Child Is Affected

Be aware if your child is teased or is asked to do things that make him look silly or different to his peers. Periodically volunteer at your school so you can observe firsthand what is happening between your child and his classmates.

Listen to other parents and identify situations that may escalate bullying. For example, sometimes children who are reading in close areas are bumped by the person sitting next to them. At other times, due to weather or scheduling, children must play inside during recess, in a small room where there is chaos, noise, and lots of movement. This can cause children to push or tease their peers, and that can cause stress on your child. Insist that your child tell you when he is frustrated at school or feels that something is wrong. Keep the communication channels open with his teacher and other parents.

Children who develop the skills of leadership and organization can use them in social interactions outside school—in parks, on playgrounds, and at social events. Facilitating language in the outside environment is the subject of the next chapter.

IN SUMMARY

- Bullying can become apparent in a preschool environment as early as the age of four. Preschool bullying is a widespread problem that compromises opportunities to learn.
- A child who develops leadership skills in preschool is likely to experience more peer acceptance in kindergarten.

CHAPTER TEN

Successfully Engaging Friends

THE MOST SUCCESSFUL PRESCHOOLERS are the ones who can engage their friends from the moment they walk in the door until it's time to leave. These are the children who are fun to be around because they seem to enjoy everyone's company. What's more, they are "present": they're paying attention, alert, and aware when they interact with their friends, and even with the adults around them.

Preschool children experience a wide range of emotions every day, and sometimes every hour. They can't be expected to be happy and engaged all of the time. However, studies show that children who appear engaged with others—who play either quietly or enthusiastically while forming relationships—achieve more success than children who don't engage with their peers. The core of preschool peer interactions and readiness to learn revealed that positive interactive play behavior is associated with active engagement in the classroom learning in preschool whereas disconnection in play related to inattention, passivity, and lack of motivation.[1]

Children who lack enthusiasm when they play with others often have difficulties in social interactions. These are the children who are wandering around the classroom aimlessly or choosing solitary play. If they don't feel that they have the skills to join others in a group

189

project, they won't join at all. Worse, they may show aggression toward potential playmates and lack close friendships.

As we've said before, children need adult assistance in order to engage other children effectively. One study Ann conducted at Clark University with her colleagues David Dickinson and Miriam Smith found that teachers who were more empathic and warm in tone were also more likely to engage children in more "cognitively challenging interactions."[2] In these higher-level conversations, the children talked about more events, shared information about the world, and discussed the meaning of words and ideas such as "what makes ice melt," rather than talked about concrete objects that were present.

This chapter will help both parents and teachers improve children's social interactions so that they become more engaged with other children. This can happen when children master more exacting language, as well as the ability to express their emotions. To accomplish this, parents and teachers need to know when the best time to intervene is and when to fade back so that the child who needs help can learn from friends. That's because the best way for children to learn how to develop more meaningful social connections is to model other children—both their siblings and peers.

THE SOCIAL PART OF YOUR BRAIN

The Enlightenment philosopher John Locke once wrote: "Let us suppose the mind to be, as we say, white paper void of all characters, without any ideas. Whence comes it by the vast store which the busy and the boundless fancy of man has painted on it with an almost endless variety? Whence has it all the materials of reason and knowledge? To this I answer, in one word, from experience."[3]

It is through experience that we learn how to be social. We learn from watching and listening to others as they perform the subtleties of making friends. We learn by experimenting with our family and peers, by using language and gestures within our own social culture.

We see others become more outgoing and empathetic, attaining a level of comfort with those around us. And if we are slow to learn on our own, we can learn how to engage with more social competence and how to relate successfully to others. It is the social and cultural experience of engaging within a conversation that leads us to feel part of a community.

In the previous nine chapters, we have explained how the brain theoretically processes many of the fundamental skills children need in order to be successful. As children use language, their brain is activated, and neural connections are being created as well as pruned. And as children form relationships, express emotions, and exhibit more executive function skills, they are making brain connections that will help them become more skilled and successful.

We also know that the brain has a unique opportunity and capacity to change during the preschool years. Although we can't prove that the brain is changed by the experience, we can recognize that change is happening. Many of the children we treat for learning or language issues improve as a result.

Some of the children we treat come to us with very basic social skills: they can use only one- or two-word phrases and can take turns only in a short interaction. Often they lack the ability to integrate all the necessary components for play, including using language appropriately and with success. Many of these children reach their potential with limited help from us, while others continue to need more assistance. Whether the social and learning experiences we create for them actually change the connections and the pathways in the brain is not confirmed.

Neuroscientists have not yet been able to pinpoint how particular neural connections communicate in order to integrate traits like personality, temperament, executive function skills, and social skills. But what is certain is that intervention can provide effective strategies to preschoolers during this critical developmental period when rapid changes are possible.

LESSONS IN ENGAGING SOCIAL BEHAVIOR

Many of the skills for social competence have already been discussed in this book: negotiation, resolving conflict, creating compromise, using language to express feelings, and seeing the perspective of others. Mastering all these skills leads to more advanced social behavior, such as becoming involved in pretend play, becoming aware of the group, and perspective taking. You may already be seeing significant changes in your child's behavior if you have begun to adopt these strategies.

Many new studies are looking at how children misperceive the social cues of others and how they become frustrated because they don't understand what their friend or a sibling is trying to tell them. By the age of three or even earlier, children should have learned to read the subtle cues of language: facial expression, body language, voice tone, and gesture. The best way to help them is to have them work with a peer or a sibling. Bring the two children close together and point out the facial expressions or body language of the peer or sibling. Stay at the children's eye level, and point out these subtle facial cues as they play. This part of socializing a child isn't easy. You must model these same expressions for your child and use a calm, warm tone of voice and respond with emotions in order to link the facial expression with meaning.

Create Story Themes That Children Can Stick With

Another technique we use to get children to engage socially is to help them pick a play theme that they can continue for an extended period of time. The story must have some coherence and be developmentally appropriate for the age of the child. An ongoing play theme allows each child to fully associate with all aspects of the character and the story. As they do, they begin to grow socially and emotionally, work out emotional issues, hold their friends accountable for behaviors, resolve conflicts, and use appropriate social rules.

In order to do this, children often need help sequencing their own ideas and logically engaging while they play and talk. As the adult, you may need to scaffold your child to help her come up with story ideas. You can help her with suggestions and then fade back once she is engaged in order to keep the story going. Typically two children approach each other and take one or two turns to request a toy or protest that they want a toy. As soon as they're close to each other, suggest to one of them that she ask her friend what she likes to do. Give both children ideas to formulate a story. Suggest a story theme with the pets, figures, or toys they'll have in their hands or are interested in at that moment.

As they begin to play, help them start the story. Suggest a sequence of actions for their play if they get stuck. Encourage them by providing suggestions only when they stop talking or retreat from each other. Stay close to them and continue to support their story ideas by repeating what they say and engaging in their story with body language, facial expression, and gestures. Point out the facial expression of each child to the other, and model their voice patterns when they are using language to express emotions.

Your child won't need this sort of support every time she engages with another child. Children remember the suggestions adults have given them and eventually read the language cues of their peer or sibling and begin to create their own sentences and their own story.

Move Children Away from Parallel Play and Toward Joint Attention

Parallel play is appropriate for toddlers. But as they reach the ages of three and four years, they begin to go back and forth between parallel play and more engagement with their friends. A preschooler usually includes one peer in play at first. They may complete a puzzle together, construct block towers together, or chase each other around the playground.

You can help make this transition easier by grouping children who have similar interests so that they are physically near each other.

Even if they're close together but playing with different objects, that's a good beginning. As they play, observe the details of the play in order to understand the story they may be creating so that you can join them as a "peer."

Then talk about the play of both children. Begin by narrating their play and describing what they are doing, and then create an extension to the story—a new idea that connects their individual play routines. For example, if one child is playing with a dump truck and the other child is pretending that he is a pilot, you can say, "Oh, I wonder if your superhero needs to make a big building for his plane. I bet Jimmy would like to help you build one." Or you can suggest that they build a landing pad on top of a building that they can construct together. You'll be surprised at your own creativity.

Keep making suggestions until the children can compromise on a new theme. One child can build a road that leads into the other child's play area. The other child can build a tower with the idea that they will include the play figures that each is holding. Together they can build a garage for their trucks and create a fire station. Or they can create a house for two fairy princesses that need a castle.

Describe the Actions of Play to Encourage Interaction

When two children are playing, they're so busy that they can forget to see another child, even if they are playing nearby. Parents and teachers can help children notice others by narrating their actions aloud.

Talk about what other children are doing as well as your own child. You can say things like, "Oh, that's a great truck. It's carrying so much lumber!" Or, "Wow. I like that truck too. You're going up a steep hill with all that sand!" By narrating the play actions, you're reinforcing the children's play themes, acknowledging that you enjoy their story and drawing attention to the other children in the room.

Be sure to stay close to both children and engage with them with gestures, facial expression, and, most important, your enthusiasm.

Keep talking about what they're doing. In just a few moments, it will become apparent that they have noticed each other's play actions.

When one peer makes a comment to the other about these actions, such as, "That's a steep hill for your truck!" rephrase the comments: "Yes, that's a steep hill!" Point to the truck's action, and then look at the other peer. If he watches his friend, keep talking about the actions: "Oh, now you are picking up all those logs! Wow. Can you make it?" The observing peer may say, "Be careful! Don't drop them!"

Then make a suggestion for both children to change their stories so that they're playing together. In this instance, the children could drive to a pretend lumberyard. You can start to build a lumberyard in between them and move another truck into the lumberyard. When you get involved directly, it's likely that they'll follow your lead and join each other.

Ask Questions Relevant to the Play

When you are playing with two or more children, it's important to create questions, which are neither invasive nor repetitive, for them to answer that will extend their play. Sometimes teachers and parents ask too many questions, and when this happens, the children immediately shut down. They will turn away, retreat, or move to the other side of the playground. At other times, adults will ask questions that have nothing to do with the play, which can divide the child's loyalty (the child may think "Am I supposed to answer Mommy and make her happy, or can I just keep playing?") and make the children confused or get off track.

The art of asking questions is almost a dance of moving in and out of the play at just the right moment. It's tricky to time the question so that you don't interrupt the flow of your child's play actions. Some researchers have criticized adult intervention with children during play because they say that children need to work out everything on their own. However, we believe that children need help in play interactions; as they get better at creating more complex stories, the adult can fade back and encourage them to ask their own questions.

Questions also provide an opportunity for the children to listen to each other's answer. This will work as long as you don't bombard a child. By asking simple questions like, "Where are we going next?" you can guide them and keep them thinking together.

Children often need help to sequence their ideas in order to stay on one story theme. Focus on questions that help them see the gestalt, or big picture of the event in the play, rather than the details. Children often get caught up in the details of their play, such as whether the wheel of their truck works or the fairy princess's wand is long enough.

At one preschool, Ann was playing with two five year olds who were making pretend cookies. Notice how Ann's questions are simple, direct, and focused on the sequence of the children's play about the cookies and ice cream:

ANN: Hey, you guys! What are you making?

DAHLIA: Chocolate chip cookie ice cream, and we're selling it.

ANN: Wow! You guys are having fun. Do you think that's really going to be good ice cream?

JILL: Yeah.

ANN: Oh, wow! Are you going to make some for your friends?

DAHLIA: We're taking turns at the party.

ANN: Oh, you're making a party. How neat.

JILL: Yes.

ANN: That's going to be nice. What kind of party is it going to be?

DAHLIA: A Halloween party.

JILL: Oh. Chocolate chip ice cream; boy, that sounds good.

ANN: This is cool. Is this your store?

DAHLIA: Yeah.

ANN: Ooh.

DAHLIA: Chocolate chip or Oreo? (Dahlia offers Ann some pretend ice cream.)

ANN: Oh, thank you. (Ann pretends to eat ice cream.)

JILL: I'll sprinkle them over here. (She adds sprinkles to the ice cream.)

ANN: Sprinkle them over, huh? Nummy.

DAHLIA: I'll mix them together.

ANN: Chocolate chip store, you guys. Great.

DAHLIA: I'll put my Oreo in.

JILL: May I please have some Oreo in mine? Can I please have some chocolate chips too?

The best part of facilitating language in play is when a child asks you to participate as a character in their story. You are "in," and that means you can then encourage their language and keep them all on track with your comments and questions. Once the child invites the parent or teacher to take a role in the story, the play becomes cohesive. The conversation will get faster, and you'll see how quickly the children engage in the story:

DAHLIA: Do you want to work here?

ANN: Sure. Can I work in your store?

DAHLIA: Sure. Ann is working with us.

ANN: Thank you for inviting me.

JAMIE: You can work with Dahlia.

ANN: Okay.

JAMIE: To sell the Oreos.

DAHLIA: You go over there.

ANN: Okay, I'll go over here and make cake.

DAHLIA: You have to take some snow, and harden it. And then there are some chocolate chips over there and vanilla.

ANN: Okay, so snow here and then chocolate chips over here. Okay.

JAMIE: We only have one customer. So I'm going to make some.

ANN: Okay, here's some cake, you guys. See if you like it. Do you want to test it? How is it? Is it good?

DAHLIA: Yeah.

ANN: Nummy, huh? Umm.

DAHLIA: Which one is nummy?
ANN: It's vanilla with chocolate icing and sprinkles on top.
DAHLIA: Umm, good job.

Help Shy Children Become More Social

Several models of play-based therapy help shy children become more socially engaged. Many of the play-based models encourage the parent or the teacher to follow the child's lead or focus on reinforcing both children with praise. However, one of our favorites is to enlist the help of a more socially skillful child.

If your child is naturally shy and reticent to approach a peer, encourage a more skilled child to join him. This provides the perfect role model to help a child become more social. Referred to as the integrated play group model, it was designed by Pamela Wolfberg for children with autism.[4] It is related to another approach, the peer buddy method, an active peer tutor training program that assigns a child with autism to a typically developing peer buddy. This peer buddy system reveals an increase in social interactions for both children, including the one without disabilities.[5] We've found great success with these strategies for typically developing children as well.

In order to encourage a sibling or friend to engage with an otherwise shy child, make sure that you praise the less skilled child and ask the more social child to respond to any initiation of play by the unskilled peer. Prompting the more social child with ideas for play shouldn't be a problem. The skillful peer can then transfer the information you give them to help the other child.

The helping friend should be encouraged to stay close to the other child so that she can hear his comments. Then prompt the helper to comment about his actions. If the less skilled child responds, praise the helper for making a relevant comment back to the child. The goal is to gain what is referred to as *joint attention*, where the two children are using language back and forth to create play and a story theme.

You can also assist by providing toys that both children love to play with. Give the toy to the skillful peer with a suggestion of how to use it. Then he can use the new toy to start the theme of the story. Designate a special area for play away from noisier peers that will promote interaction. This play space can be defined with an area rug or by organizing the toys in one part of a room.

Work with Narrative Play Therapy

Ann's method of play therapy, which you have seen in the dialogues throughout this book, is called narrative play (NP).[6] In the NP model, parents and teachers learn how to engage children with peers and facilitate language between them. This method develops a child's skills in three domains: language skills, play skills, and narration or storytelling skills. Although this therapy was created for children with a range of learning issues, it can also be effectively used with typically developing children.

The first phase of NP is *first contact*. The goal for the parent or caregiver or teacher is to make contact and begin a relationship, even if it is only to imitate your child's gestures and sounds. The phase 1 child lacks the ability to use language to engage and recruit others. She may have no language except for overt gestures, noises, and sometimes crying and often pulls her parent's hand and points to what she needs and wants. The child uses toys or objects by manipulating them but shows limited ability to use symbolic play by representing a real-life object with an inanimate object—for example, using a twig from a tree as a wand. Her play is limited, or she may not be able to play at all. This child may be isolated, fearful, and unable to create a story or to even notice others. During this phase, the adult observes, listens, and acknowledges the child's actions and follows and imitates the child in whatever he may be doing.

In the second phase of NP, *joint attention*, the child becomes more aware of others. She uses some reciprocal relating by looking at a toy and then up to the parent or other adult and back (an eye-gaze shift) and often uses language to request and protest when things are frustrating. This child uses limited language along with pointing. The phase 2 child is learning how to construct towers and play objects with the adult and to stay near them. She is learning how to engage with simple comments about what they are doing. In phase 2, the child is starting to tell a simple story with objects and use symbolic play. As symbolic play develops, her language develops almost at the same time. Once she relates to another person and shares some play event, such as building together, the parent can introduce the child to a peer or put them together with a more skilled sibling.

Language becomes important in this phase as the child begins to use words to express emotions, use gestures related to what is being said, and use symbolic play to pretend with objects in play. In this phase, you can encourage your child to run with a friend; however, you should stay close to the two children so you can make comments while they play. You can model for both children by making comments and narrating their actions in play.

The phase 2 child imitates her peers, follows others, and is aware of others as she plays. She no longer just collects objects in boxes or dumps them out and returns them to the same box. She shares them with others and looks at peers and joins them in play. She wants to be near his peers.

In the third phase of narrative play, *child-initiated reciprocity*, a child learns to respond to one peer and talk back and forth, making comments and sharing an event in play. A sibling or a peer can be taught to describe the actions or the feelings and sounds and images of what is happening as they play. For example, if they are outdoors at a pond, the peer can point to a tall pine tree and say, "Look at that tree. It bends with wind!"

The adult needs to join them and say, "Oh, look how the wind is blowing across the pond!"

Then the peer might respond by saying, "Yeah. Look at the ripples! They look like tiny waves."

Sometimes the ducks themselves can provide a prompt for a child by quacking and swimming along a wind-blown pond. The child and playmate can run along the shore of the pond and talk to the duck.

Once Ann was with two children watching a duck swim at Walden Pond in Concord, Massachusetts, when one child said to the other, "Wow. He is a fast swimmer! Look at his legs paddling. Look how he swims! Let's try to keep up with him!"

Finally, the child moves into the fourth phase of narrative play: *social engagement*. The phase 4 child can create a rhythm to her play as she talks to playmates peers at the same time. She chatters to others about her play and their actions. She makes connections to others easily. Her facial expressions, body language, and gestures match what she is saying. If she is a pretend pirate on the playground, she is motioning to the others to follow the ship and moves her arm to keep them running with her toward their goal. She is reciprocal in her actions and use of words. She uses language to express ideas and emotions and is learning to problem-solve and negotiate. In this phase, the parent or the teacher is fading back as the child learns to socialize and play with several other children. Language expression, emotion, and telling stories become an integral part of the back-and-forth exchange in play. In this final phase, language, play, and narration are completely interconnected in a seamless whole.

Here is how one group of five year olds in phase 4 of narrative play acted. They were playing with water and sand outside their pre-school and talking about building a house they could live in. One child jumped up from the sand, threw his arms up, and announced, "Okay, I'm the architect. We can build our house right here!" Another child yelled, "Yes, and we can have a bedroom over here." A third child immediately grabbed some buckets, passed them out to the other players, and said, "Let's build!" The excitement of the group was clear. They all begin to build, watching each other, talking about their "room," and helping each other. No teacher supported their story, until the moment when two children wanted to build the same bedroom and began to quarrel. The teacher stopped them, and helped them figure out how to resolve this conflict. Once they decided that they want to be "friends forever," they agreed to share a bucket and build one room together.

Foster Taking Turns

Games and sporting activities are essential for preschoolers and promote social play. They help children become aware of each other as they engage in a game, encourage them to talk to each other, and help them maintain a strong relationship with a friend as they share an event. This type of play is critical for the natural development of a child in cognitive (thinking and reasoning) skills, social interactions with peers, and an understanding of how to join a community of other children.

Successful play isn't complicated. Children love to engage in simple, clear games that keep them moving and talking. Socially engaged children can wait for a turn, resist the temptation to grab a desired object, and clean up or make a transition to end an activity without resisting. These skills are all part of executive function, which we discussed in Chapter Eight, because they involve working memory and sensory integration. They can be reinforced with simple activities, such as playing catch or hot potato. Children playing catch in a group have to wait for the ball, and they need to control their excitement while they are waiting. When they get the ball, they must name the next person and throw the ball to that child without hesitation. When it is time to move to another outside game, they learn to stop and move on.

Other skill-building games children can play include throwing beanbags into a target that has been made with chalk on the playground or the wall of a building. They can line up with a few peers, wait for their turn, get the beanbag, and toss it toward the goal in hopes that it will end in the center spot. Or they can use the chalk to draw intricate pictures—pretend cities or maps of the playground—with each other. They can all walk around and view each other's drawings and talk about them.

A simple obstacle course helps children learn to take turns and follow directions. All you need are a few hula hoops placed strategically

A TRAVELING GAME BAG

The tools you need to play simple games are good to keep in your car when you are on the go. You can prepare a bag with a few materials that are age and size appropriate for your child. For example, most preschoolers do not have the capacity to sit through a long board game like Shoots and Ladders or even Candy Land. We find that they prefer quickly paced card games, such as Slamwich. Preschoolers love to slam their hand down when they put down their three cards and discover the sandwich. The duffle bag can include

- A jump rope
- A timer
- Small soccer balls
- Sponge ball and bat
- Baseball gloves (small)
- Helmet for batting
- Plastic bases
- Card games like Slamwich
- Toy cars and figures
- Soft (Gertie) ball
- Cones to mark fields
- Beanbags and chalk
- Wind-up toys

around the playground or a large room. Children can try hopping from one to the next. All of the children will have to wait for a turn, control their hopping and jumping, and regulate their bodies as they move from one to hoop to the next. These hoops can also be used as targets or for exercise. If your child needs to expend some extra energy, take her outside, and tell her to jump in and out of the hoop thirty times.

Modify Team Games

Playing team games should be fun for all the children involved. As a child engages in team games and sporty play and talks with her friends, she learns to negotiate, express and regulate emotions, reason logically when explaining her ideas, and think about the ideas of others. As she makes more connections with her peers, she learns to be more flexible, more organized, and more compassionate. Yet many preschoolers cannot engage in a full-blown soccer game or endure the fast pace of the kicking and passing of quick and skilled peers. They may need a modified soccer game to be able to socially engage.

Instead of sticking hard and fast to the official rules, you can set up a simple soccer field by placing four plastic cones at four corners in a reasonably sized area. Then show the child how the game is played. Preschoolers need to be pretaught the rules for soccer, baseball, or any other game where team members participate all at once. An adult can use a poster board or a table, place small figures, and practice the basic rules of the game. An adult must remember that many preschoolers don't know they will need to kick the ball toward their own goal on the other side of the field. Once when Ann was teaching a group of five-year-old boys to play soccer, one of them promptly kicked the ball into the goal he was standing in front of—the other team's goal. That was a moment for laughter and learning.

Baseball is another team game that can be modified easily for this age group and adapted into other team games such as kickball. The bases need to be close, and the rules can be customized so that they don't have to focus on forced outs, which can actually confuse a young child. A preschooler understands what it means to be tagged out but not when she is "out" because another team member ran to the next base. This takes time to learn.

OUTDOOR SETTINGS INTERESTING TO PRESCHOOLERS

Preschoolers love to be outdoors where they can be free to run, construct stories, and pretend. The world outside is full of surprises, presents new challenges, and has fewer rules than indoor environments, where play tends to be more structured and predictable. When we watch most children, we can see that they love to be near nature—in the woods, at a farm with animals, or on a playground.

As a parent or teacher, our job is not only to bring children outdoors, but to stimulate them socially. They need to be in outdoor settings with their friends. Bringing your child outdoors with a friend can entice the children to listen and focus on the big picture, able to explain the emotions and the overall gestalt of experiences rather than the details. Researchers who study preschool play behavior have found that children are more likely to take part in the most complex type of peer play (interactive dramatic play) in an outdoor setting rather than indoors.[7] In outdoor play, children interact more with peers, create more intricate pretend stories, and engage more in resolving conflicts. Children playing outdoors show more enthusiasm and are present in the moment. They are more alert to what is happening around them and know when their play with peers is reciprocal and meaningful.

Making some connections with nature such as watching animals, gazing up at the sky, watching leaves change color in the fall, looking at rippling water in a stream, collecting rocks, and taking hikes in the mountains or playing in powder snow are events that capture a young child's imagination. Integrating some of these experiences into family life is essential for the physical and emotional health of children. New studies say that exposure to nature can reduce the symptoms of attention deficit hyperactive disorder and can also help children's cognitive abilities and resistance to stress.[8]

Choosing Outdoor Locations Wisely

Young children love to bring home treasures, but at most farms, the owners don't want children to take anything away from the natural environment and deplete the rocks and twigs on the ground. The teachers and parents need to find materials such as rocks, twigs, and recycled materials that are thrown away or available to teachers. Some companies provide these materials to teachers for free. When they visit farms with animals or ponds with small beaches, they collect stones, sticks, and other small objects and use them in play at the area, but they keep them there for next time. A large branch from a neighbor who is cutting down a tree can become a complete dollhouse with pretend tables, chairs, and beds. The parent may need to help cut the branch into smaller pieces to create the "furniture." Look for pine cones and pine needles that are on a trail where children can bring them home and then these can turn into art projects at school.

Preschoolers also love to visit the real world where their heroes work every day. An excellent outing is the local fire station, where they can wear a firefighter's hat and even climb into a fire truck. Usually the fire department has special days for preschoolers to visit. Talk about these experiences, and take photographs. Make books on the computer so they can share with grandparents, friends, or classmates. Back at home or in the classroom, they can talk about what firefighters do and create stories about them in their play.

Pick-Your-Own Orchards

Preschoolers like to pick fruit from trees or bushes or from the ground. Strawberries are easy for little hands to grasp. So are blueberries and raspberries that grow on bushes at their height. Apple, pear, or peach orchards are fun because they offer a big expanse to run around, but the children require adult help in picking the fruit off the tree.

At any of these locations, have children share buckets with their friends. This is a great way to encourage children to relate to each other. There will be many opportunities for them to share ideas, talk about the fruit, and notice the details of what is happening around them. As they walk, the children can talk to each other and you can point out interesting aspects of the scene. Children make social connections as they observe what is happening in the world outside their home or their classroom. For example, many apple orchards have a farmstand or a place where children can watch a farmer tap the trees for maple syrup. At the farm stand, they can watch the staff sell fruits, vegetables, bread, and candy.

The Beach

Shallow tide pools at the beach or near a pond offer exciting opportunities for children to explore safely. Assign each child a buddy, and show them where to search for shells or sea objects. If the tide is low, the children will discover many objects to collect. You can encourage peers to show each other their special sea objects and describe them. You can also help create language between peers or siblings by making comments such as, "Look what Tommy has! It is a huge shell that has so many colors!" By modeling this comment, you will encourage the children to make their own comments. When the children begin talking to each other, the adult can fade back and let them play with each other in the tide pools. The most important part of such a trip can be the social interactions between the children.

A Farm

One advantage of taking children outdoors is that the environment itself facilitates vivid and descriptive language and social interactions. A farm is one of the best places to help children become more social and use descriptive language with emotions. They can talk about the animals, talk to the animals, and share their comments with each other.

For preschool children, the sight of chickens, horses, pigs, goats, sheep, snakes, and flowering trees that rise to the top of the red barns is dramatic. These images entice them to talk and run toward what they see. The children hear the sounds of the animals, the tractor, the hayride truck, the farmworkers, and other children. The outdoors at a farm is a place to engage with friends.

Ann was visiting Drumlin Farm, the Massachusetts Audubon Society's working farm in Lincoln, Massachusetts, with several preschoolers. When they entered the chicken house, a large rooster began to crow. The children all laughed and covered their ears from the loud sounds.

Ann asked, "Who can make that sound?" They all tried and laughed even harder. When they entered the pigpen and saw six piglets and a very large pink mother pig covered in mud, the children all covered their faces.

Ann commented, "Whew! They are smelly!"

As the children got on the bus to go home, they remembered and retold the story of how the rooster was loud and the pigs were so smelly. The sounds of the rooster and the image of the huge muddy pig, as well as the smell of the farm, stayed with the children all day long. They talked about the farm visit at school, to their classmates, and at home with their family. The farm became the most important socializing part of their day.

TIPS FOR ENCOURAGING SOCIAL ENGAGEMENT IN PLAY

The following strategies and tips help children and parents engage in outside conversation in natural settings. The tips will help children join each other in play and socially engage with peers.

Follow Your Child's Lead and Allow Him to Point Out What Is Happening in the Play or at an Outside Event

Most preschoolers love to run around a new park or a new situation and point out what is happening. As they run and point, follow them. This simple activity helps you make a quick connection to what they are interested in and also gives you many opportunities to reinforce their language and describe details. You can make comments and notice what they are pointing out.

Identify Children Who Are Social and Might Be Helpful to Your Child as They Play

When planning your child's play dates, pick friends you think will be calm, organized, and able to use social language appropriately to express their emotions. This is a delicate issue. Sometimes your child will want to play with a child who is the opposite: defiant, unregulated, loud, and disorganized. If your child is adamant about playing with difficult children, take them to a movie where the goal isn't social interaction. It is important for your child to be around more socially skilled peers who can help him become more social.

Help Children Approach Others, but Only When Needed

Some preschoolers may need you to take them by the hand, walk them toward a new peer on the playground, and stay with them until they show you that they are comfortable. Others may need you to make the initial contact for them and then quickly fade back and stay out of the interaction. The most socially advanced children will go off on their own, ready to make their own friends. Each of these situations requires a parent to know his or her child's comfort level.

Once the children are engaged and following each other, you can stay close, observe, and move in to help only when you see a potential problem in the play. Monitor and give positive instructions, and guide the children with your own affect, your genuine praise, and your engagement with them.

Engage in Age-Appropriate Play

Be sensitive to your child's age, and use developmentally appropriate language. Don't give your child social scripts that may be younger or older for their age group. Suggest language that they can use easily for their skill level. For example, if your child is three years old, suggest that she initiate play by asking, "Can I play? Can I have a turn?" If your child is four years old, suggest language that is more complex and shows that the child is more aware of what other children are doing, such as, "Can I do that too? What are you making? Can I help?"

By the time a child is five years old, you can suggest that she use more linguistically complex language (longer complex sentences, with more grammatical changes and embedded clauses), such as, "Oh, John and I want something to do to make that airport." A three year old might say, "Can I see that airport?"

The initiation by a five year old to join peers has to be more advanced and show that he recognizes the whole story and the play of the peers. In addition, be sure that your child is using play that is appropriate and interesting to others. Preschoolers love to pretend, and they create story themes that are relevant to what they feel is important to them in the moment. Be sure to recognize these interests when you make suggestions.

Preschoolers also need to play alone: they can't be socially engaged all the time. The goal is for your child to become independent and monitor his own interactions in play, so that others will find him socially engaging. As children engage in the outdoors, they see the world outside their home and their classroom and become a part of the larger community. They understand more about how the world includes many cultures, many types of children, and many new environments.

Children carry the images of the outdoors back home and can talk about them at school, or create interesting projects about their world. All of this helps them become more social and more successful.

IN SUMMARY

- Children learn to be social with support through watching and listening to others as they engage in the subtleties of making friends.
- Children become aware of each other as they engage in games and play. Encourage them to talk to each other, and help them maintain a strong relationship with another child as they share an event.

CHAPTER ELEVEN

Become Passionate About Learning

SUCCESSFUL CHILDREN ARE PASSIONATE about the world around them. They are curious explorers at home, in the classroom, and at the park. They ask questions and expect answers that give order and reason to their lives. They respond immediately to any environmental changes, wanting to know where a noise is coming from, or why there is a sparkling light on the wall as the wind moves the curtains, or who is coming to their house.

Curious children find ways to investigate everything around them and ask question after question until they have an answer that satisfies their interest. These preschoolers turn curiosity into a passion for learning, discovering, and creating.

When children are passionate about learning, they are also creative, and not just with crayons or art projects. They see the world through a creative lens and apply it to their friendships, play themes, and relationships with parents and teachers. They can invent characters or ideas almost out of nowhere. They are in a happy state, both alone and with a peer, enjoying what they are engaged in and allowing their language and the story to flow.

This chapter explores how creativity facilitates language in a playful way so that children develop passion as they learn with others.

SHARING CREATIVITY

When children create, they know that they have made something special. They want to share it, whether their activity was planned or not. Once Ann asked a preschooler, "How did you make that so fast?"

The child answered, "I made it because I'm happy. See, it's beautiful!"

You can almost see the wheels moving inside the heads of passionate children. Their faces shine when they come up with an answer that pleases them. Most important, they are fun to be with because their passion is contagious.

Creating from Passion

One day during a swirling nor'easter snowstorm in Massachusetts, several children were playing outside their preschool, creating what the teachers thought was going to be a wide and very thin snowman. The children patted the snow together while they jumped up and down with laughter, taking breaks by running around it. One child seemed to be the leader and added direction to the event. He said, "Okay, over here, we need more snow! Okay, Jimmy find the sticks! Lucy, find the bark for the eyes!" Light snow was falling as they finished up their creative project. They were thrilled.

The teacher said, "Okay, let's get a hat for his head and some bark for his buttons!"

The children all turned at once and stopped their snow building. The leader child said to the teacher, "It's *not* a snowman. It's a snow horse! We need sticks for the reins and bark for the nose and his eyes! We need some leaves to make the saddle! Then we can ride it!" The children continued to run around their horse until they finished their work.

We love this story because it shows how children can harness their creativity: they have their own ideas about their world and know what it takes to create whatever they desire. Often as teachers and parents, we forget to allow children to be creative. Yet access to creativity and the ability to express ideas in new and different ways is at the core of what it means to be successful.

Allowing Children to Be Creative

Creativity encompasses sensitivity, fluency, flexibility, originality, elaboration, risk taking, and, of course, imagination. Children who are creative not only come up with new questions; they come up with the answers. What's more, their unique ideas motivate them to finish any task that helps them solve a problem.

Curious and creative children are successful because they are willing to risk failing at their own tasks so they can create what they imagine to be the best in their mind. If they enjoy ice cream, they may want to make their own version of ice cream, real or pretend. Even if their experiment doesn't work well, they want to try it. And they will persist until they get a chance to make that ice cream. Many educators and researchers say that this motivation to create something and finish it is more important than intelligence when it comes to early childhood success.[1]

CREATIVITY AND THE BRAIN

The brain is not a linear, orderly, predictable system.[2] Rather, it's dynamic and subject to frequent change. A child's brain is processing information constantly about what he sees, how he feels, what he must organize, how he must inhibit certain responses, how he controls his emotions, how he uses language to express his ideas, and how he tells a story or answers a question. And each person's brain is doing this in a completely unique way through its system of attention and filtering. People file important things away as memories; but others see the same information as extraneous, and they quickly forget it. These decisions, often made on a millisecond timescale, are what make each of us unique and may influence our capacity for creativity.

This filtering process is how the brain creates distinct and novel neuronal connections that are forming the pathways. At the same time, the brain is functioning to monitor more basic body functions and movements. Motor skills, auditory processing, visual input, and other sensory activity are all organized and regulated with individual differences. This is what makes some of us faster than others, but it also influences our sensitivity to the world around us.

The question now is how a brain organizes itself to be more, or less, creative. The latest research confirms that sometimes both sides of the brain are involved in many human activities. Researchers originally thought that the left side of the brain is activated when using language, and that it processes information in a logical and sequential order. The right side was considered to be more visual, processing information intuitively, holistically, and randomly. Now when neuroscientists map language activity, we can see that both sides of the brain are activated.[3]

Scientists thus far have only hunches as to where true creativity comes from. Many artists talk about finding themselves in a zone of creativity that for them is easy to harness but more difficult to repeat on demand.

What we can quantify is the time we allot children to be creative. We can provide the right physical tools for creativity, as well as the emotional support they need. Children must be given the opportunity to be curious and the chance to make mistakes without retribution so that they can feel comfortable enough to take risks that will lead to new ideas, art, or friendships. When children know that they are safe to create something and will not be criticized for making "mistakes," they will be eager to try new things and learn new skills.

PASSION FOR EXPLORATION BEGINS AT HOME

Many children are naturally creative. Some children like to be creative with toys, environmental objects (sticks, mud, tree leaves), or arts and crafts. Others create complex stories with interesting plots by playing with words. Still others are creative in the way they develop relationships with peers.

You can begin to foster creativity at home by taking a distinct interest in your child's play. You can say, "I notice that you're really curious about what's happening." Or, "You're quite clever about thinking about different ways to play with your friends." By encouraging him, you are telling the child that he is clever and creative.

Allow children to use everyday materials in unusual ways without showing them the "right" way to do things. Jenifer Demko, a preschool director Ann works with, tells a story about a child who was pasting her painting on a piece of paper. The expectation was that she was going to put the glue under the image and put the image down and complete the task. However, she proceeded to put a thorough coat of glue across the paper. When it dried, it had a crispy, crackly coat that made the drawing shiny and wonderful. Because no one directed her work and said, "Don't put the glue over there!" the girl created something novel and beautiful.[4]

Creativity Happens with Interesting Materials

Creativity happens when children are given interesting materials to work with and the time to play together with these materials without a set of rules or structure. Creative ideas and language flow as children engage in play with others, particularly if an adult who joins them is as fully engaged as the children.

Once during a play period, Ann joined a group of four year olds at a water table filled with glue, water, sequins, Valentine hearts, lots of sparkles, and tiny glass jewels. Five children surrounded the table, each with her or his hands dipped into the "Valentine soup." Ann supported their creative thinking and their creative play by rephrasing what they said, using her own affect to engage with them as a peer would, and by helping them share and explain their feelings about the glue and the sparkly water.

ANN: Oh, you've got to tell me what you're making.
CARA: Soup.

ANN: You're making soup.

MAX: Yeah! Valentine Day soup!

ANN: What kind of Valentine Day soup is this?

CARA: Hearts Valentine soup!

ANN: Isabel, what are you using to make it?

CARA: Some slime and water and glitter and some thingies—like this stuff. (She holds up some globs of sparkles and glitter.)

ANN: Some slime and some glitter and some water and some sparklies and some . . . what is that all over your hand?

CARA: Glue.

ANN: Is it glue and glitter?

CARA: Yeah. It's all cold water.

ANN: It looks like fun, and I like all of those sticks you have with hearts. Oh, what did you find? It looks like you found jewels, right? Ooh, look at that. Make sure you share. Cara needs some. Max needs some. What's that? Those look like frozen hearts. Are they frozen hearts?

CARA: Yeah, they're really frozen hearts.

ANN: Ooh, they're cold. Do you think that your teacher made them in the refrigerator?

CARA: Yeah. Save me some.

ANN: Oh, this is really beautiful soup. Wow, this soup is so beautiful. Do I get to try it out? Do you think I can eat it?

MAX: Nooo.

ANN: Why not?

MAX: Because of the glitter and the sugar and the dirty water.

CARA: With all that gooey stuff that I made.

MAX: And these thingies.

ANN: What are those thingies? Those are jewels, huh?

CARA: And you can eat this.

MAX: I have to really wash my hands. This is messy, slimy, and stuffy.

ANN: It's really, slimy, stuffy, huh? Oh, look at this squishy stuff.

In the middle of this Valentine soup project, Ann asks Nicole to talk about the actions of another child. This helps Nicole notice what a classmate is doing and encourages them to engage with each other.

Ann points out the heart and how she's putting it on a spoon, which brings the child's attention to a detail that is related to a peer. As you see here, a *peer* announces what the child is doing with the small heart.

ANN: What's she doing? She's carrying an ice heart over into the soup. Look what she's doing again.

NICOLE: Making some soup.

ANN: She's making soup, but what is she doing with the heart? Nicole, what is she doing with the heart?

NICOLE: She's pouring it in with a spoon.

ANN: That's pretty funny.

NICOLE: You have to eat all of it.

ANN: What would happen to me if I eat all that soup?

CARA: You'll die.

ANN: No! That would be sad. I don't want to die. I want to live. I think living is fun.

NICOLE: Well, get back in your car and go drive to Florida.

CARA: Drive to Florida, and you'll never be able to come back. They won't give you the directions.

ANN: Oh, you won't give me the directions to come back here. That would be so sad. I would miss you guys.

NICOLE: You have to eat all of it. Let's just get the gooey stuff.

CARA: No, that stays in there.

ANN: That's really good. Oh, yummy. Well, I'm back from Florida now. I'm living again. Okay, I'm going to have a little taste of this one. Whoa! Look at this. I found the biggest heart jewel there is and an "I love you" sign. Thanks, Cara. That's delicious.

Later that day one of the preschoolers announced to Ann, "I'm glad you didn't go to Florida!"

Passionate and Creative Children Ask Interesting Questions

Children who are passionate about learning are curious by nature and can create their own fun. If there are small items on a table, some children will approach their teachers and immediately create a game or project with each other. These children think of options in play and create objects that are in their own mind. They love to create new stories or think of new things to make.

Other children rely on their parents or teachers for setting up their play or answering their questions. Typically these children will move from one activity to the next with the announcement, "Hey, Mom, what can we do? I'm bored!" Although there is nothing wrong with this behavior, parents get into the routine of solving the problem for their children without letting them explore their own options.

These children need to be taught how to answer their own questions instead of always checking in with an adult. A bored or less inquisitive child might walk over to a play area, pick one toy, bring it to the teacher, and say, "I don't know what to do!" Your best response is, "What do *you* want to do?"

One preschool teacher we know, Beth Ann Boelter-Dimock, tries to connect the task a child is thinking about to something that he already knows and get him to wonder what's possible.[5] This means that the adult needs to first find out the child's interests. He may be interested in Star Wars or Harry Potter, or making fairy houses or fire stations. You must make the right suggestions to the child that take his interests into consideration and then watch his facial expression. If the child smiles, he is interested in the idea.

Then suggest that he create something around the subject that he loves. Prompt him to ask himself, "Okay, what does a fire station look like? Are there trucks with ladders and hoses? Are the trucks near the station or in the station? What does this building look like?"

Then the adult can ask the child, "So if the fire trucks have tall ladders, how can you make them? What do you need to make a fire truck? Can you use this cardboard box and these sticks?" As the child moves into the project and begins to create something, the adult can guide him with praise and suggestions.

When he creates something that doesn't look like what you think it should, ignore your thoughts and praise him for his creation. As the child answers his own questions, he will begin to ask his own. He may ask, "I wonder where the firemen sleep?" or "I wonder if they have a real kitchen and if they eat food?" The more a child gets excited about asking himself a question and finding his own solution, with some help from the adult, the more he will implement this task again on his own without any help. Children become more curious once they know that their answers will be accepted. Then encourage them to go off and explore those answers.

Creative Children Are Good Problem Solvers

Preschoolers need to be reminded to solve their own problems, express their ideas, and acknowledge the shared interest they have in being together. A creative teacher takes this time to be with children when they disagree, guiding them by talking it through with them and helping them see options for addressing the problem. Preschoolers need guidance from adults, but they also need their own power to create questions about what they are doing and the clarity to make their own decisions about their play and friendships.

In the following interaction, two five year olds approach a teacher and want her to resolve their problem. Instead of doing the work for them, the teacher asks them to talk about how they feel. She allows them to solve the problem by giving them creative ideas.

BETH: What's the problem?

ANDREW: (crying) He wants me to change my mind. I didn't want to hear that. He wants me to play something else, and I didn't want to!

BETH: Oh, so you have another idea of what to play?

NICO: Yes.

BETH: Well, that's okay. You're still friends. Right?

ANDREW: But we always have to play Star Wars.

BETH: I think yesterday you played other things. Maybe you forgot.

ANDREW: I don't like Star Wars!

NICO: I wanted to build a ship.

BETH: Well, what can you guys do? What's the solution to this problem? I know you're sad. But what's going to make you feel better?

ANDREW: He's trying to make me change my mind.

NICO: I'm not trying to change his mind.

BETH: You know why he's talking to you, why he's saying these things:
he likes you. He wants to play with you. You're fun to play with. So
do you want to do something different or play the same thing?

NICO: Okay, we can do something different. (The two boys go off and
play together.)

The teacher was able to remain calm, be at the two children's eye
level, show her own concern, and listen to their worries. As they
explained how they felt, she introduced the idea that they cared about
each other. With this turning point for both children, they immediately decided to play together and create a whole new story.

TIPS FOR ENCOURAGING CURIOSITY AND CREATIVITY

The following strategies and tips help parents and teachers
provide safe and creative materials to help children be more
creative and be able to see other options to traditional projects.
These tips include ways to use music, photography, and art to
engage with children and encourage language interactions.

No Matter What Your Child's Creative Project May Look Like, Don't Assume That Your Child Is Creating What You Have in Your Mind

Don't try to steer her to create what you think the project ought
to be. Allow your child to think of her own options, even if
her ideas aren't traditional. If she picks up a stick, don't tell her
what you think the stick represents. Wait until she tells you.

Allow Play to Include Any Kind of Materials as Long as They Are Safe

If the child wants to play in mud and he has the right mud clothes on (all children should have clothes for playing in mud), let him play. He may create mud castles, or forts, or something he imagines. Encourage free play whenever possible with objects from the environment. Arrange art materials in bins with easy access. Allow him to use environmental objects like sticks, rocks, and dirt to create story themes. Don't worry about how dirty he will become in the process.

Broaden Your Child's Experience by Going to New and Exciting Places

We strongly believe that an adventure is just outside your door. When you take your child to new places, you are allowing her to have a host of new experiences. But when you go, try not to rush through the event. Spend time at these places and let her explore. Follow her, and have fun. Don't rush back because you haven't cleaned the garage or worked on your bills or fixed the roof. This time with your child is precious and critical to her development.

Here are a few suggestions:

- A pottery place where children can play with clay and create sculptures. This is a great activity to do at home as well because clay is relatively easy to clean up.
- Go out to lunch at restaurants that are child friendly. Allow your child to try new foods she shows interest in, even if you think she won't like them. Order a few appetizers instead of large dishes so that you can share and compare what you like and what you don't like to eat.
- Take your child with you on errands. We all know that it is always easier to leave your child at home (attended, of course) instead of dragging him to the airport or the

supermarket. But these activities not only give you an opportunity to show him new places and new experiences; they give you something to talk about together. Once you are doing an errand together, make the most out of it. For example, if you are at the market, buy ingredients so that you can cook or bake together.

Encourage Your Child to Engage in Music and Be Creative with Sounds

Music and song help children develop language in creative ways. If you have a drum, give the child a drumstick, and create new tunes with rhythm as you tap the drum. When you use new words, extend the vowels and play with the sounds. This will encourage the child to be more creative in the words she chooses to use in a conversation. You can also use drums to encourage dance and rhythm. You can use a drum, either a large ocean drum that has beads inside or a simple drum with a mallet for tapping it. Tap out sentences that she likes. She will imitate you and practice syntax (word order). For example, you can say, "I love Lily! She likes me!" and tap the syllables out on the drum. She will follow you; when she creates a good sentence on her own, imitate her words. Reward her by rolling the beads inside the drum. You can use a small piano to play simple songs and sing with her. Teachers might include song and practice using sentences in their class. Children love rhythmic chants to move from one play area to the next. Hand clapping with chants also helps children change activities.

Give Your Child a Scrapbook and Take Photos When You Go Outside

This exercise helps children notice the details and engages their curiosity and creativity. Allow them to take pictures of anything they want. Most children love to see themselves in photos, and once they do, they may want to create a special way to display their pictures. Even if you are not a photographer, you can take simple photos, and your child will carry them around, talking to everyone about his adventures.

When children can make the emotional and linguistic connections among language, play, and storytelling, they are ready to become good learners. These three aspects of brain and social development merge so children can engage in the classroom in a meaningful way. This typically happens between three and five years of age.

By adding skills like creativity and curiosity to the mix, you are preparing your child to embrace learning and at the same time feel good about himself. When children start to link play with learning and can use language to express their ideas and emotions (and at times even contain them), everything comes together: you've got a successful child.

IN SUMMARY

- Many educators and researchers believe that a child's motivation to create something and finish it is more important than intelligence when it comes to early childhood success.
- Parents and teachers must allow young children to follow their own ideas, not just their parents' preconceived ideas.
- Storytelling is a great vehicle for helping children become more creative in their thinking.

CHAPTER TWELVE

Successful Children Need Involved Parents

THROUGHOUT THIS BOOK, we have identified skills that are apparent in children who are successful: they are likable, happy, advanced in their thinking, have a strong moral character, are resilient, are ready to compromise, are organized, know when to be a leader, and can engage enthusiastically with their peers. Children with these skills are usually expressive, creative, enthusiastic, and motivated to learn. They love to be social with other children as well as adults, and they are inspired to create objects that are novel and interesting.

Some children naturally have many or all of these skills. They are the ones who can make sophisticated connections and remember what you said to them a week later. When they see you, they want to talk to you and be with you.

Yet preschoolers are not always well behaved or successful. Some children may not be comfortable with eye contact. They may have a flat expression, or may be shy, or not yet advanced in using language. But we believe that these children also have the potential to be successful. Given the right opportunity, they can learn how to be more engaged with other children, which will help them acquire many of these other characteristics.

PUTTING OUR STRATEGIES INTO PRACTICE

You now have the tools to identify and address issues that may be affecting your child's social or academic performance. Your child may fall anywhere on the continuum of social development. By addressing, modifying, and supporting his development at this critical time of brain plasticity, you are creating the best opportunity for change.

The late child pediatrician and psychiatrist D. W. Winnicott believed that parents don't have to be perfect to raise healthy, happy children. We couldn't agree more. We all know that no parent is perfect, just as we know that no child is perfect. However, there are small changes you can make in the way you relate to your child that will make an enormous difference in her later success.

Be Present and Involved in Play

The most important way you can encourage your preschooler's social development is to get more involved in all aspects of her life, especially in their play. This will give you the opportunity to see how successful your child is with other children. And if she is not doing well, you can step in and facilitate a change in her behavior.

By getting involved in play, you are also creating a special relationship with your child that will last a lifetime. Your child will see you not only as a parent but as a person who is genuine and concerned: she will pick up that you want to know how she feels, what she believes in, and how she plays with her friends. This is important groundwork to set up, because young children deeply want and need their parents to be close, to know what they are doing, and to join them in their world. As they get older and prefer to hang out with their friends instead of you, it will become more difficult for you to join in.

Although it is important to play with your preschooler one-on-one, it's equally critical to enter your child's play when she is with a friend. Our strategies and tips can help you quickly redirect a negative play situation, and put your child and her friends back on the right track. Join the children by doing whatever they are doing. Don't constantly ask, "Who can I be?" Instead, pick up your own play object, perhaps a toy figure or a fire truck, and suggest a role for yourself in their story theme.

Focus on Ten Core Strategies

Aside from being involved in play, the strategies and tips we've outlined in the book may not always be appropriate or necessary for your child. However, we've found that the following ten strategies apply to many children, most of the time. These are the concepts that we instill in the parents we work with, who use them constantly when they interact with their children. If you can remember to incorporate these into your daily life, you'll find that your child will be more engaged with you, and that's the first step to success.

1. Model genuine emotions with clear affect, using facial expressions and appropriate language that conveys how you feel.
2. Talk about the children's actions and ideas instead of drilling them with questions.
3. Physically get down to their level, and follow them so that they can see your expressions, hear your language suggestions, and make eye contact.
4. Use world situations as an opportunity to teach moral development.
5. Identify and share the positive aspects of a negative event.
6. Keep a sense of humor.
7. Help children find a shared interest in order to come to agreements.
8. Use the natural environment as a tool to engage your child in creative activities.
9. Assess your child's emotional state, and plan the day accordingly.
10. Be mindful of bullying and how your child is affected.

Whether you engage with your child at home, at the playground, at a farm, or in the child's classroom over a water table filled with Valentine soup, you will be making a significant difference in her chance to be successful later in life.

Children Are Always Listening and Working Out Their Fears

Children do listen to what you say and how you say it. They are watching how you move, your gestures, and all of the other subtleties of language, whether you are talking directly to them or to someone else. That is why it is critical to be aware of how you present yourself and the information that you share with them.

The following conversation between Ann and a group of girls who are pretending to get married is a perfect example. We don't know how these children arrived at their story theme. Perhaps these girls were watching a television program, or maybe one was listening to adults talking. We do know that sometimes children use dramatic play to work out their fears. When this happens, you need to be ready to extend the discussion if the story turns into a negative event.

ANN: Hi, Lexi. What are you doing?

LEXI: Hi. I'm playing.

ANN: Are you going to become something? Do you need some help?

LEXI: I'm going to marry a bad guy.

ANN: You did what?

LEXI: I and my children marry a bad guy.

ANN: You guys are going to marry a bad guy? Together?

LEXI: Yeah.

ANN: That's kind of interesting.

LEXI: A really bad, bad guy.

ANN: And what are you going to do with this bad, bad guy?

LEXI: I'm going to marry him and dance with him.

ANN: Why would you want to marry a bad guy?

LEXI: I don't know.

ANN: Wouldn't you want to marry a good guy who is nice to you?

LEXI: Nah.

ANN: Oh you guys are too funny. What are you doing now? Are you going upstairs?

LAUREN: We're going to the wedding on the elevator.

ANN: And when you come down, you'll be married?

LAUREN: Yeah. I'm up, up way upstairs. You got to get out of here.

ANN: Oh, okay. I'd better get out of the way. Is this the elevator?

REMI: All right. Let's go out.

LAUREN: She's going to marry the bad guy.

ANN: Well, then what happens to them? Are they pirates or something?

LEXI: They come home with us.

ANN: Okay. So what happens to you after you're done being married? Then what are you going to do?

REMI: Go home. Go on a honeymoon.

ANN: Oh, really. Then what?

REMI: Then we'll be nice to each other. We know how.

ANN: Oh, really. Like how will you be nice?

REMI: We're going to make dinner for each other and go out for coffee.

ANN: Anything else?

REMI: Yes, we'll take care of each other. We won't let anyone be mean.

OUR BEST TOY ADVICE

We believe that every child needs some unstructured play time during each day to choose toys to play with and be allowed to explore, either alone or with a friend. It's perfectly acceptable to allow your child to play on his own. However, he should have some time with other children during each week. If he has siblings, it is very important to encourage him to play with them as well as to have alone time.

There are only a few rules for picking out toys for children. In our opinion, the best toys are the ones that engage an existing interest. If your child likes playing with dolls, buy dolls that show different ethnic features or ones that reflect the many stages of physical development. If your child likes dinosaurs, provide a variety of shapes and sizes. Don't worry if your child gravitates toward toys that might be what others perceive as gender specific. If your daughter likes trucks, encourage her to play with them.

Whatever your child's interest, make sure to choose toys that are safe to play with and are age appropriate. If the toy is teaching a concept important for the child's developmental level, it is fine. If it is far above his level, it is not helpful.

Encourage your child to choose toys that he can be creative with and share with peers. Find toys that your child's friends love so your child can feel included in the larger group's play. This isn't a license to buy toys that you are morally opposed to (say, guns or swords) just because other children play with them. And more important, don't be afraid to limit play with a particular toy if it turns out to be too dangerous or creates a negative experience with a peer.

If your child insists on playing with Star Wars light sabers, for example, that's fine as long as he engages in a pretend combat rather than create a story where he physically assaults a friend with the toy. The children can pretend to be Star Wars characters, but they need guidance. If the toy of choice is a machine gun and you know that your child is obsessive about pretending to kill all his peers, it may not be a good purchase. Use your own intuition, and guide your child in the best way you can. And most important, don't be afraid to change your mind and take a toy away if it is physically or psychologically harmful.

Choose toys that are created from recyclable materials or are handmade from elements you can find in your own back yard. You can collect natural objects for later pretend play or art projects. A long stick might become a great wand for a fairy princess; pine cones can be wonderful building objects for pretend small houses. Preschoolers love to create things out of old wood to make a birdhouse, or find sticks to use for building or making a pretend fire in the woods.

When children use these objects to represent real life objects in play, they are using symbolic play, one of the cornerstones to advancing language development. The child will have to think about what the object looks like and will need to be creative and expand her story theme to incorporate it into her play. Once Ann was watching two preschoolers pile up sticks and rocks on the edge of a pond. They sat down near the pile and proceeded to create a pretend summer camp together. They danced around the "fire" and built shelters with their rocks. They talked to each other, created a story, and played for hours.

Encourage children to play with toys that allow them to be creative. In order to facilitate dramatic play, choose dolls or action figures they can use to role-play their stories. Your old clothes can be used for costumes so your child can take on different roles. Preschoolers love to be a "fire chief" with a big red hat, or a "school teacher" with a small blackboard and some chalk, or a "mother" with a baby doll and pretend milk bottles and baby food. Hanging an old curtain can help create a space to use for a stage where the children can perform stories. You can provide a pretend microphone or even a simple stick so the story can have an announcer.

Invest in toys that promote open-ended play or ones that can keep a story theme going over several play dates. Children will remain engaged in their story if you add new objects to the play area that relate to what they already show an interest in playing with. For example, children love to pretend that they are cooking or having a birthday party. If you already have a kitchen set, you can add small plates, forks, pretend food, and a table with a table cloth. They may even bake a great cake and invite you to the party.

In general, we've found that preschoolers love to play with

- Squishy balls
- Doll houses or play sets with figures
- All modes of transportation: planes, trains, trucks and cars, tracks, garages, gas stations, airports, railroad stations

- Wind toys that spin and jump
- Art supplies of all types: clay, crayons, stickers, sparkly glitter, and glue
- Blocks and boxes to build houses and forts
- Dress-up clothes
- Play utensils for a kitchen and pretend food
- Cash registers for a pretend store
- Small musical instruments

COMPUTERS AND ELECTRONIC GAMES

Research is not yet conclusive as to whether new technologies and television, including home theaters, provide interference for a young child's language development or contribute to learning. This is not a license to leave your child in front of the television or a computer and walk away, however. As researchers Daniel Anderson and Tiffany Pempek report, if the extensive exposure to television has a negative impact on young children, "We should try to understand what we are doing and what the consequences are."[1] While television programming may not be helpful or harmful, it is important to consider the amount of time that a preschooler spends with electronic media. We know that any expectation of real learning from television for young children, particularly under the age of two, is poor and cannot be compared to what that child will learn from you or her preschool teacher.

We have found that a few electronic toys successfully teach social engagement, the alphabet, or phonics skills. In general, we do support "child development" computer games, such as the software programs and applications that can be downloaded onto an iPhone or iTouch. We don't support videotapes, DVDs, or computer software that is not backed up by research or reviewed by teachers and parents.

The following software programs for preschoolers have high customer ratings (4.5 to 5 stars overall), and we have also used them with preschoolers, with some success. They can all be downloaded from the iTunes store to an iPhone or an iPod touch, and they are either free or inexpensive:

- Baby Flash Cards-2, by Dream Cortex
- iZoo Free, iZoo for Toddlers, iZoo (talking with wild animals), by Todd Matheson, Matheson Software (also available in French, Russian, Spanish)
- Peekaboo Barn version 2.0, by Night & Day Studios (also available in Spanish)
- iWriteWords version 2.7 (a tracing game), by PT. Global Dinamika
- I See Ewe: A Preschooler Word Game version 1.5.1, by Michael Kamprath (also available in Chinese, German, and Spanish)
- Infant Arcade: Alphabet Creatures version 1.3.1, by Iskandar
- Infant Arcade: Numbers Lite version 1.1, by Iskandar
- Letters A to Z from True Learning version 1.1, by Refresh Media
- Alphabet Air from True Learning version 1.0, by Refresh Media
- Kids Finger Painter version 1.0.2, by Jose Villegas, Third Frame Mobile
- Bumblebee Touchbook version 1.1, by EDAL
- Itsy Bitsy Spider by Duck Duck Moose, version 1.0.1
- Wheels on the Bus by Duck Duck Moose, version 1.0.4
- Tozzle Lite-Toddler's favorite puzzle version 3.0 by Benjamin Riegler, Herbert Blaha

SUCCESS HAPPENS WHEN PRESCHOOL AND HOME CONNECT

You are the key to your children's success, both in and out of the classroom. We strongly believe that parents must make an effort to communicate with their children's teachers and form a strong bond between home and school. This communication is one of the foundations for successful children. If a parent understands what the teachers are doing to encourage social engagement in the classroom, then the child can be practicing the same lessons at home and at school. Parents and teachers need to collaborate and often make a formal plan for what works best for each child.

If a parent meets regularly with the child's teacher, they can fill each other in, including how the child's play dates are going or how the child is interacting within the family. The teacher can also provide insight into the situation and share new ideas on how to engage the child with peers outside the classroom.

Teachers need the support of the parents, and more than many parents understand. For example, sometimes a child may be active and running around the classroom, bumping into play objects or other peers. The teacher may need to limit the child by saying, "Jimmy, be careful. You need to walk in the classroom." The child may go home and complain that his teacher was "mean" to him today. If the parent and the teacher have a good working relationship, they can clear up this miscommunication. The parent will realize that the teacher wasn't being mean at all, only setting limits. The parent can also support the teacher by reminding the child not to run inside spaces that are close, like classrooms or small hallways.

At the same time, parents and caregivers need all the support they can get from their child's teachers. Sometimes teachers forget what parents go through every single day with young children. Parents are often exhausted from the everyday activities of their own lives or the lives of their other children. They also tend to view their child's individual issues as monumental, where a teacher might see the same behavior as average or typical. Teachers are in a unique position to help parents take some of this pressure off and teach them realistic expectations of preschool behavior.

WE HOPE IT ALL COMES TOGETHER

With time and commitment on your part, we are fully confident that these well-honed strategies do work together to make a difference in your child's overall success. The following story is one of our favorite examples.

When we started treating Tracey, she was just four years old and shy, timid, and unable to engage in preschool. On the first day of school, Tracey looked around the classroom at the other children and immediately grabbed her mother's leg and yelled, "Take me home!"

In the days that followed, her mother was heartbroken to leave her screaming child on the teacher's lap. The teacher would hold Tracey for the first two hours, hugging her and trying to distract her with toys that might help her recover from the separation. Nothing seemed to work until one day, Tracey discovered a small chicken coop near the playground, which was located on an apple orchard farm.

It was spring, and the newborn baby chicks were outside in a bin, heated by tiny lights. The children gathered around the lights, chatting and pointing toward the baby chicks. Tracey was afraid of the chicks at first and climbed into her teacher's lap. She watched her peers and finally stopped crying, slid down from her teacher's lap, and ran toward the baby chicks. Her smile and laughter could be heard across the playground. She cried, "Look, they're so cute!" Tracey spent the next week sitting quietly by the baby chicks, even when it was raining. The teachers stayed close to her and encouraged her to talk with the mother hen, even though Tracey wouldn't talk to anyone in the classroom.

One day Ann joined Tracey near the chicken coop, sitting near her side, but not too close. Tracey smiled at Ann and asked, "Do you like them?" Ann nodded back to say yes, and asked, "Do you want to touch one?" Ann picked up the mother hen. Tracey began to pet her feathers. They sat together as a gentle rain fell. The teachers just watched.

For two more weeks, Ann sat with Tracey for an hour each morning as she pet the mother hen and pointed out the baby chicks. Tracey began to talk to the mother hen, to the baby chicks, and finally to Ann. By the third week, Tracey wanted to share her experience with a classmate. Ann brought over a boy named Charlie, whom she chose because Charlie was calm and a good talker. Charlie pointed to one chick that was chirping and said, "Tracey, he's scared. See, he's shaking." Tracey looked up at him and giggled. Ann told them, "Sometimes when you're brand new, you feel scared. Right?" Tracey nodded her head to say yes.

Over the next several months Tracey started to relate to her peers. She was shy at first, but Ann continued to join her, narrating her actions in play and helping her see what the other children were doing in the classroom. Ann talked about her friend's feelings and used affect and emotions. She continued to relate back to the tiny baby chicks, which were also becoming more social. Ann encouraged Tracey to be the weather person at circle time so she could announce when the rain was coming and the animals needed to be put in the barn.

After a year of social skills training with Ann and lots of time spent with her classmates in play, Tracey transformed into a self-confident leader who was truly ready for kindergarten. Later she became an excellent reader and a socially adjusted first grader.

Not every child will make this change and be as successful as Tracey has been. But many children do make this leap and become social when they learn how to be comfortable with their peers.

We can attribute Tracey's transformation to many different parts of her own life, including her innate tenacity to learn, but mainly to her wonderful teachers and her parents who wanted to help her become more successful. They followed many of the strategies we've outlined in this book, encouraging Tracey to move beyond her shyness and to play with her classmates. In fact, Tracey's bond with Charlie remained for many school years.

Today Tracey is a leader in her local community. She is an accomplished litigation lawyer who graduated from a prestigious Ivy League university. And she still remembers the days when she screamed in preschool and finally sat quietly with the baby chicks. In every way, Tracey's life can be considered a success, and she knows that part of her achievement started with a little help from her parents and teachers back in preschool.

We wish you and your child the same success.

Notes

Introduction

1. Diamond, A., and Amso, D. "Contributions of Neuroscience to Our Understanding of Cognitive Development." *Current Directions in Psychological Science*, 2008, *17*(2), 136–141, p. 136. The research was done at Weill Cornell Medical College, New York City, July 29, 2008.

2. Shonkoff, J., and Phillips, D. (eds.). *From Neurons to Neighborhoods: The Science of Early Childhood Development*. Washington, D.C.: National Academy Press, Jan. 2007.

3. U.S. Department of Education, National Center for Education Statistics. *The Condition of Education*. Washington, D.C.: U.S. Department of Education, 2007.

Chapter One

1. Gopnik, A. *The Philosophical Baby*. New York: Farrar, Straus and Giroux, 2009.

2. Klingberg, T. *The Overflowing Brain*. New York: Oxford University Press, 2009, p. 11. Klingberg talked about brain plasticity at a conference at MIT: Modern Brains, Enhancing Memory and Performance in This Digital Distracting Age, Nov. 20–22, 2009.

3. Goldsmith, H. H., Pollak, S. D., and Davidson, R. J. "Developmental Neuroscience Perspectives on Emotion Regulation." *Child Development Perspective*, 2008, *2*(3), 132–140.

4. Klingberg, *The Overflowing Brain*, p. 11.

5. Engel, S. "Playing to Learn." *New York Times*, Feb. 1, 2010.

6. Singer, D. G., and Singer, J. L. *Imagination and Play in the Electronic Age.* Cambridge, Mass.: Harvard University Press, 2005.

7. Berk, L. E., Mann, T. D., and Ogan, A. T. "Make-Believe Play: Wellspring for Development of Self-Regulation." In R. M. Golinkoff and K. Hirsh-Pasek (eds.), *Play = Learning.* New York: Oxford University Press, 2006, pp. 74–100.

8. Thompson, R. A. "Development in the First Years of Life." In E. F. Zigler, D. G. Singer, and S. J. Bishop-Josef (eds.), *Children's Play: The Roots of Reading.* Washington, D.C.: Zero to Three Press, 2004, pp. 15–31.

9. Singer, D. G., and Singer, J. L. *Imagination and Play in the Electronic Age.* Cambridge, Mass.: Harvard University Press, 2005.

10. Berk, Mann, and Ogan, "Make-Believe Play."

Chapter Two

1. Schaaf, R. C., Schoen, S. A., Smith Roley, S., Lane, S. J., Koomar, J. A., & May Benson, T. A. "A Frame of Reference for Sensory Integration." In P. Kramer and J. Hinojosa (eds.), *Frames of Reference for Pediatric Occupational Therapy.* (3rd ed.) Philadelphia: Lippincott Williams and Wilkins, 2010. This definition was also developed from a discussion with Teresa May-Benson, ScD, OTR/L, research director of the Spiral Foundation and clinical director of OTA-Watertown, and Ann Densmore in Feb. 2010.

2. Ayers, J. *Sensory Integration and the Child.* Los Angeles: Western Psychological Services, 1994.

3. Kranowitz, C. S. *The Out-of-Sync Child Has Fun: Activities for Kids with Sensory Integration Dysfunction.* New York: Perigee Books, 2003.

4. Quoted in Goldsmith, H. H., Pollack, S. D., and Davidson, R. J. "Developmental Neuroscience Perspectives on Emotion Regulation." *Child Development Perspectives*, 2008, *2*, 132–140, p. 136. This is a study on brain chemistry and biology.

5. Kagan, J. *The Long Shadow of Temperament*. Cambridge, Mass.: Belknap Press of Harvard University Press, 2004, p. 244. This text was taken from Dr. Kagan's book, and the paragraph was developed from an e-mail discussion between Ann Densmore and Dr. Jerome Kagan on Sept. 16, 2009.

6. Kagan, *The Long Shadow of Temperament*, p. 3.

7. Kagan, *The Long Shadow of Temperament*, p. 5.

8. Landa, R. "Assessment of Social Communication Skills in Preschoolers." *Mental Retardation and Developmental Disabilities Research Review*, 2005, *11*, 247–252.

9. Gopnik, A. *The Philosophical Baby*. New York: Farrar, Straus, and Giroux, 2009, p. 55.

10. Gopnik, *The Philosophical Baby*, p. 58.

11. Greenspan, S. I. *The Challenging Child*. Reading, Mass.: Addison-Wesley, 1995; *First Feelings: Milestones in the Emotional Development of Your Baby and Child*. New York: Penguin Books, 1985; *Child with Special Needs: Encouraging Intellectual and Emotional Growth*. New York: Perseus Books, 1998; Greenspan, S. I., and Weider, S. *Engaging Autism*. Cambridge, Mass.: Da Capo Press, 2006.

12. Katch, J. *Under Deadman's Skin: Discovering the Meaning of Children's Violent Play*. Boston: Beacon Press, 2001; "Soap Won't Do the Trick." *Teacher Magazine*, 2001, *12*(5), 52–53; and "The Truth Behind Violent Play," *Independent School*, 2001, *60*(4), 86–91. Chang, N. "Reasoning with Children About Violent Television Shows and Related Toys." *Early Childhood Education Journal*, 2000, *28*(2), 28. Greenspan, S. I. "When a Child's Play Themes Are Violent." *Scholastic Early Childhood Today*, 2006, *21*(3), 24–25.

13. Ann Densmore, June 10, 2009, interview with Janet Craig, a preschool teacher with a master's degree in child development, at the Children's Meeting House in Concord, Massachusetts.

Chapter Three

1. Elkind, D. *The Power of Play*. Boston: Da Capo Press, 2007.

2. Ginsburg, H. P., Inoue, N., & Seo, K. H. "Young Children Doing Mathematics: Observations of Everyday Activities." In J. V. Copley (ed.),

Mathematics in the Early Years. Washington, D.C.: National Association for the Education of Young Children, 1999.

3. The discussion on play research in early childhood as a precursor for academic success was developed from Singer, D. G., Singer, J., Plaskon, S., and Schweder, A. "A Role for Play in the Preschool Curriculum." In S. Olfman (ed.), *All Work, No Play: How Educational Reforms Are Harming Our Preschools*. Westport, Conn.: Praeger, 2003. See also Singer, J. L., Singer, D. G., and Schweder, A. E. "Enhancing Preschoolers' School Readiness Through Imaginative Play with Parents and Teachers." In R. Clements and L. Fiorentino (eds.), *The Child's Right to Play: A Global Approach*. Westport, Conn.: Greenwood Press, 2002.

4. *Guide to U.S. Department of Education Programs 2009*. Washington, D.C.: Office of Communications and Outreach.

5. Humphries, C. "Untangling the Brain: From Neuron to Mind." *Harvard Magazine*, 2009, *11*(5), 40–46.

6. Bredekamp, S. "Play and School Readiness." In E. F. Zigler, D. G. Singer, and S. J. Bishop-Josef (eds.), *Children's Play: Roots to Reading*. Washington, D.C.: Zero to Three Press, 2004.

7. Dickinson, D. "Large-Group and Free-Play Times: Conversational Settings Supporting Language and Literacy Development." In D. Dickinson and P. Tabors (eds.), *Beginning Literacy with Language: Young Children Learning at Home and School*. Baltimore, Md.: Paul H. Brookes, 2001; and direct quote from David Dickinson in an e-mail conversation between Ann Densmore and David Dickinson, July 2010.

Chapter Four

1. Miller, S. "Helping Happiness Along: I Love It!" *Scholastic Early Childhood Today*, 2007, *21*(7), 30–35.

2. Berk, L. E., Mann, T. D., and Ogan, A. T. "Make-Believe Play: Wellspring for Development of Self-Regulation." In D. G. Singer, R. M. Golinkoff, and K. Hirsh-Pasek (eds.), *Play = Learning*. New York: Oxford University Press, 2006.

3. Berk, Mann, and Ogan, "Make-Believe Play." Children weave into their self-talk or private speech a rich tapestry of voices from their social

world. Wertch, J. *Voices of the Mind: A Social Cultural Approach to Mental Action.* Cambridge, Mass.: Harvard University Press, 1993.

4. Berk, Mann, and Ogan, "Make-Believe Play," p. 82.

5. Broderick, N. Y. "An Investigation of the Relationship Between Private Speech and Emotion Regulation in Preschool-Age Children." *Dissertation Abstracts International: Section B: The Sciences and Engineering, 61*(11–B), 2001, 6125.

6. Berk, Mann, and Ogan, "Make-Believe Play."

7. Klingberg, T. *The Overflowing Brain.* New York: Oxford University Press, 2009, p. 11.

8. Nelson, C. A. "Neural Development and Lifelong Plasticity." In R. M. Lerner, F. Jacobs, and D. Wertlieb (eds.), *Handbook of Applied Developmental Science.* Thousand Oaks, Calif.: Sage Publications, 2002.

9. Jerome Kagan, personal interview, Nov. 2009, regarding temperamentally inhibited children. See also Kagan, J. *The Long Shadow of Temperament.* Cambridge, Mass.: Harvard University Press, 2004.

Chapter Five

1. Catherine Snow discusses the way parent-child interactions define right versus wrong and the concepts of good versus bad. "Comment: Language and the Beginnings of Moral Understanding." In J. Kagan and S. Lamb (eds.), *The Emergence of Morality in Young Children.* Chicago: University of Chicago Press, 1990. See also Dunn, J., Bretherton, I., and Munn, P. "Conversations Between Mothers and Young Children About Feeling States." *Developmental Psychology*, 1987, *23*, 132–139.

2. Brody, J. "Empathy's Natural, But Nurturing It Helps." *New York Times*, Feb. 15, 2010.

3. Greenspan, S. *The Challenging Child: Understanding, Raising, and Enjoying the Five "Difficult" Types of Children.* Reading, Mass.: Addison-Wesley, 1995.

4. Dunn, J., Bretherton, I., and Munn, P. "Conversations Between Mothers and Young Children About Feeling States." Snow, "Comment."

5. Schieffelin, B. "Getting It Together: An Ethnographic Approach to the Study of the Development of Communicative Competence." In E. Ochs and B. B. Schieffelin (eds.), *Developmental Pragmatics*. Orlando, Fla.: Academic Press, 1979.

6. Peterson, C. C., and Siegal, M. "Changing Focus on the Representational Mind: Deaf, Autistic and Normal Children's Concepts of False Photos, False Drawings and False Beliefs." *British Journal of Developmental Psychology*, 1998, *16*(3), 301–320.

7. Baron-Cohen, S. *Mindblindness: An Essay on Autism and Theory of Mind*. Cambridge, Mass.: MIT Press, 2001.

8. Pinker, S. *The Language Instinct*. New York: Penguin Books, 1994.

9. Blair, R.J.R., and Blair, K. S. "Empathy, Morality, and Social Convention: Evidence from the Study of Psychopathy and Other Psychiatric Disorders." In J. Decety and W. Ickes (eds.), *The Social Neuroscience of Empathy*. Cambridge, Mass.: MIT Press, 2009.

10. Decety, J., and Lamm, C. "Empathy Versus Personal Distress: Recent Evidence from Social Neuroscience." In J. Decety and W. Ickes (eds.), *The Social Neuroscience of Empathy*. Cambridge, Mass.: MIT Press, 2009.

11. American Academy of Pediatrics. "Media Education." *Pediatrics*, 1999, *104*, 341–342. This article was discussed in the following paper presented at the Modern Brains conference at MIT, Nov. 20–22, 2009: Anderson, D. R., and Pempek, T. A. "Television and Very Young Children," *American Behavioral Scientist*, 2005, *48*(5), 505–522.

12. Anderson and Pempek, "Television and Very Young Children."

13. Paley, V. G. *A Child's Work: The Importance of Fantasy Play*. Chicago: University of Chicago Press, 2004, p. 100.

14. Weissbourd, R. *The Parents We Mean to Be*. Boston: Houghton Mifflin, 2009.

15. Greg Mortenson is the cofounder of the nonprofit organizations, the Central Asia Institute and Pennies for Peace (www.penniesforpeace .org). He established many schools in rural and volatile regions of Pakistan and Afghanistan, which provided education for more than twenty-eight thousand children where no education opportunities existed before. His book *Three Cups of Tea* has been adapted for young readers: Mortenson, G., and Relin, D. O. *Three Cups of Tea: One Man's*

Journey to Change the World . . . One Child at a Time (adapted by S. Thomson). New York: Puffin Books, 2009.

Chapter Six

1. Werner, E. E., and Smith, R. S. *Vulnerable but Not Invincible*. New York: McGraw-Hill, 1982.

2. Kagan, J. *What Is Emotion?* New Haven, Conn.: Yale University Press, 2007.

3. Smeekens, S., Riksen-Walraven, M. J., and van Bakel, H.J.A. "Cortisol Reactions in Five-Year-Olds to Parent-Child Interaction: The Moderating Role of Ego-Resiliency." *Journal of Child Psychology and Psychiatry*, 2007, *48*(7), 649–656.

4. McCready, A. "For Some Parents, Shouting Is the New Spanking." *New York Times*, Oct. 21, 2009. Amy McCready, the founder of Positive Parenting Solutions, teaches parenting skills and coaches parents in an online course.

5. Ann Densmore, interview with Marilyn Walsh, teacher at the Apple Orchard School, and her class, 2009.

6. Communication with Yaniv's family on Jan. 15, 2010, by e-mail, about their ideas on how they maintained a sense of family security in the middle of a war. The family visited the United States several times a year and for two years, they stayed in residence in Cambridge, Massachusetts. They placed their son, Yaniv, in a private preschool in Brighton, Massachusetts. Ann traveled to the preschool twice a week to work with Yaniv in his school environment. In addition, he came to her office once a week with his family for speech therapy and consultation.

Chapter Seven

1. Fisher, R., and Ury, W. *Getting to Yes: Negotiating Agreement Without Giving In*. New York: Penguin Books, 1981. This section was developed as a result of a conversation between Ann Densmore and Bruce Patton, cofounder and distinguished fellow of the Harvard Negotiation Project,

one of three authors of *New York Times* best-seller, *Difficult Conversations*. New York: Penguin Books, 1999.

2. Smith, J., and Ross, H. "Training Parents to Mediate Sibling Disputes Affect Children's Negotiation and Conflict Understanding." *Child Development*, 2007, *78*(3), 790–805. Smith and Ross are researchers in the Department of Psychology of the Family Studies Laboratory of the University of Waterloo in Ontario, Canada. They found that parent mediation training sessions had beneficial effects on children's conflict understanding and their conflict interactions.

Chapter Eight

1. Gioia, G. A., Espy, K. A., and Isquith, P. K. *Brief-P: Behavior Rating Inventory of Executive Function-Preschool Version*. Lutz, Fla.: Psychological Assessment Resources, 2003.

2. Garon, N., Bryson, S. E., and Smith, I. M. "Executive Function in Preschoolers: A Review Using an Integrative Framework." *Psychological Bulletin*, 2008, *134*(1), 31–60.

3. Garon, Bryson, and Smith, "Executive Function in Preschoolers"; Sartre, M., Gehring, W., and Kozak, R. "More Attention Must Be Paid: The Neurobiology of Attentional Effort." *Brain Research Reviews*, 2005, *1*, 145–160.

4. Mesulam, M. M. "The Human Frontal Lobes: Transcending the Default Mode Through Contingent Encoding." In D. Stuss and R. Knight (eds.), *Principles of Frontal Lobe Function*. New York: Oxford University Press, 2002, pp. 8–30.

Chapter Nine

1. Trawick-Smith, J., "Let's Say You're the Baby, Okay? Play Leadership and Following Behavior of Young Children." In *Young Children*. Washington, D.C.: National Association for the Education of Young Children, July 1988, pp. 51–59. Jeffrey Trawick-Smith, professor at the Center for Early Childhood Education at Eastern Connecticut State University, has investigated the process by which preschoolers develop leadership.

2. Klingberg, T. *The Overflowing Brain*. New York: Oxford University Press, 2009.

3. Frey, K. S., Hirschstein, M. K., Edstrom, L. V., and Snell, J. L. "Observed Reductions in School Bullying, Nonbullying Aggression, and Destructive Bystander Behavior: A Longitudinal Evaluation." *Journal of Educational Psychology*, 2009, *101*(2), 466–481.

4. Craig, W. M., and Pepler, D. J. "Observations of Bullying and Victimization in the School Yard." *Canadian Journal of School Psychology*, 1997, *13*(2), 41–59.

5. Craig, W. M., and Pepler, D. J. "Understanding Bullying: From Research to Practice." *Canadian Psychology*, 2007, *48*(2), 86–93.

6. Frey, K. S. "Reducing Playground Bullying and Supporting Beliefs: An Experimental Trial of the Steps to Respect Program." *Developmental Psychology*, 2005, *41*(3), 479–491.

Chapter Ten

1. Coolahan, K., Fantuzzo, J., Mendez, J., and McDermott, P. "Preschool Peer Interactions and Readiness to Learn: Relationships Between Classroom Peer Play and Learning Behaviors and Conduct." *Journal of Educational Psychology*, 2000, *92*(3), 458–465. Coolahan is the head of Mathematica Policy Research in Princeton, New Jersey; John Fantazzo and Paul McDermott are professors at the Graduate School of Education, University of Pennsylvania; and Julia Mendez is professor in the Department of Psychology at the University of South Carolina.

2. Densmore, A., Dickinson, D., and Smith, S. "Socio-Emotional Aspects of Teacher-Child Interactions in Preschools." Paper presented at the annual conference of the American Education Research Association, San Francisco, Apr. 22, 1995.

3. Locke, J. *An Essay Concerning Human Understanding*. New York: Dutton, 1947. (Originally published 1690.)

4. Wolfberg, P., and Schuler, A. L. "Integrated Play Groups: A Model for Promoting the Social and Cognitive Dimensions of Play in Children with Autism." *Journal of Autism and Developmental Disorders*, 1993, *23*, 467–489.

5. Bass, J. D., and Mulick, J. A. "Social Play Skill Enhancement of Children with Autism Using Peers and Siblings as Therapists." *Psychology in the Schools*, 2007, *44*(7), 727–735.

6. Densmore, A. *Helping Children with Autism Become More Social: Seventy-Six Ways to Use Narrative Play*. Westport, Conn.: Praeger, 2007.

7. Shim, S-Y., Herwig, J. E., and Shelly, M. "Preschoolers' Play Behaviors with Peers in Classroom and Playground Settings." *Journal of Research in Childhood Education*, 2001, *15*(2), 149–163.

8. Louv, R. *Last Child in the Woods*. Chapel Hill, N.C.: Algonquin Books, 2008.

Chapter Eleven

1. Kyung-Hwa, L. "The Relationship Between Creative Thinking Ability and Creative Personality of Preschoolers." *International Education Journal*, 2005, *6*(2), 194–199.

2. Andreasen, N. C. *The Creative Brain: The Science of Genius*. New York: Penguin, 2005.

3. Andreasen, *The Creative Brain*.

4. Ann Densmore, interview with Jenifer Demko, director of the Cambridge Ellis School, Cambridge, Massachusetts, Mar. 2010.

5. Ann Densmore, interview with Beth Ann Boelter-Dimock, teacher and former professor in early childhood at Northeastern University and Lesley College in Boston, currently teaching at the Friends School in Cambridge, Massachusetts, Feb. 2010.

Chapter Twelve

1. Anderson, D. R., and Pempek, T. A. "Television and Very Young Children." *American Behavioral Scientist*, 2005, *8*(5), 505–522.

Additional Resources

Books

Apel, K., and Masterson, J. *Beyond Baby Talk: From Sounds to Sentences—a Parent's Complete Guide to Language Development*. Roseville, Calif.: Prima Publishing, 2001.

Barbarin, O. A., and Wasik, B. H. *Handbook of Child Development and Early Education, Research to Practice*. New York: Guilford Press, 2009.

Bilmes, J. *Beyond Behavior Management: The Six Life Skills Children Need to Thrive in Today's World*. St. Paul, Minn.: Redleaf Press, 2004.

Borba, M. *Parents Do Make a Difference*. San Francisco: Jossey-Bass, 1999.

Brazelton, T. B., and Sparrow, J. D. *Touchpoints: Three to Six*. New York: Da Capo Press, 2001.

Brown, S. *Play: How It Shapes the Brain, Opens the Imagination and Invigorates the Soul*. New York: Penguin, 2009.

Charlesworth, R. C. *Understanding Child Development*. (8th ed.) Belmont, Calif.: Wadsworth, 2010.

Coles, R. *The Moral Life of Children: How to Raise a Moral Child*. Boston: Houghton Mifflin Company, 1986.

Coloroso, B. *The Bully, the Bullied, and the Bystander*. New York: HarperCollins, 2008.

Crystal, D. *How Language Works*. New York: Penguin, 2005.

Derman-Sparks, L., and Olsen Edwards, J. *Anti-Bias Education for Young Children and Ourselves*. Washington, D.C.: National Association for the Education of Young Children, 2010.

Elkind, D., and Faculty of Tufts University, Eliot Pearson Department of Child Development. *Proactive Parenting: Guiding Your Child from Two to Six*. New York: Berkeley Books, 2003.

Everly, Jr., G. S. *The Resilient Child*. New York: DiaMedica Publishing, 2009.

Garabedian, H. *Itsy Bitsy Yoga for Toddlers and Preschoolers: Eight-Minute Routines to Help Your Child Grow Smarter, Be Happier, and Behave Better*. New York: Da Capo Press, 2008.

Greenspan, S. I. *First Feelings*. New York: Penguin Books, 1985.

Hirsh-Pasek, K., Golinkoff, R. M., Berk, L. E., and Singer, D. G. *A Mandate for Playful Learning in Preschool*. New York: Oxford University Press, 2009.

Hirsh-Pasek, K., and Golinkoff, R. M., with Eyer, D. *Einstein Never Used Flash Cards*. New York: Rodale, 2004.

Kagan, J. *The Nature of the Child*. New York: Basic Books, 1984.

Karp, H. *The Happiest Toddler on the Block: How to Eliminate Tantrums, and Raise a Patient, Respectful and Cooperative One- to Four-Year-Old*. New York: Random House, 2008.

Kirp, D. L. *The Sandbox Investment: Preschool Movement and Kids First Politics*. Cambridge, Mass.: Harvard University Press, 2007.

Klass, P., and Costello, E. *Quirky Kids: Understanding and Helping Your Child Who Doesn't Fit In: When to Worry and When Not to Worry*. New York: Random House, 2004.

Kranowitz, C. S. *The Out-of-Sync Child Has Fun*. New York: Perigee, 1998.

Levin, D. E. *Combating the Hazards of Media Culture*. Washington, D.C.: National Association for the Education of Young Children, 1998.

Levin, D. E. *Teaching Young Children in Violent Times: Building a Peaceful Classroom*. Washington, D.C.: National Association for the Education of Young Children, 2003.

Lickona, T. *Character Matters: How to Help Our Children Develop Good Judgment, Integrity, and Other Essential Values*. New York: Simon & Schuster, 2004.

Louv, R. *Last Child in the Woods*. Chapel Hill, N.C.: Algonquin Books of Chapel Hill, 2008.

McCartney, K., and Phillips, D. (eds.). *Handbook of Early Childhood Development*. Oxford: Blackwell, 2006.

Nelson, E., Erwin, C., and Duffy, R. A. *Positive Discipline for Preschoolers: For Their Early Years—Raising Children Who Are Responsible, Respectful, and Resourceful*. New York: Three Rivers Press, 2007.

Olfman, S. *All Work and No Play: How Educational Reforms Are Harming Our Preschoolers*. Westport, Conn.: Praeger, 2003.

Paley, V. G. *The Boy Who Would Be a Helicopter*. Cambridge, Mass.: Harvard University Press, 1990.

Paley, V. G. *You Can't Say You Can't Play*. Cambridge, Mass.: Harvard University Press, 1993.

Paley, V. G. *The Classrooms All Young Children Need*. Chicago: Chicago University Press, 2009.

Paley, V. G. *The Boy on the Beach: Building Community Through Play*. Chicago: University of Chicago Press, 2010.

Pantley, E. *No Cry Discipline Solution*. New York: McGraw-Hill, 2007.

Scarlett, G. W., Naudeau, S., Salonius-Pasternak, D., and Ponte, I. *Children's Play*. Thousand Oaks, Calif.: Sage Publications, 2005.

Shapiro, L. E. *Learning to Listen, Learning to Care: A Workbook to Help Kids Learn Self-Control and Empathy*. Oakland, Calif.: New Harbinger Publications, 2008.

Singer, D. G., Golinkof, R. M., and Hirsh-Pasek, K. *Play = Learning: How Play Motivates and Enhances Children's Cognitive and Social-Emotional Growth*. New York: Oxford University Press, 2006.

Wolfberg, P. J. *Play and Imagination in Children with Autism*. New York: Teachers College Press, 1999.

Youngs, B. B., Wolf, J., Wafer, J., and Lehman, D. *Teaching Kids to Care*. Charlottesville, Va.: Hampton Roads Publishing Company, 2007.

Zigler, E. F., Singer, D. G., and Bishop-Josef, S. J. *Children's Play: The Roots of Reading*. Washington, D.C.: Zero to Three Press, 2006.

Blogs

About Parenting Preschoolers, www.preschoolers.about.com

Excellence in Early Childhood, http://preschoolprofessional.blog

Learning Is Child's Play, www.learningischildsplay.blog

Little Fingers That Play, www.littlefingersplay.blog

Literacy in the Block Center, www.preschoolknowledge.blogspot.com

Our Preschool Homeschool Blog, http://ourpreschoolhomeschool.blogspot.com/

Pre-K Pages, www.pre-kpages.com/blog1/

Preschool Playbook, www.preschoolplaybook.com/

Top 50 Blogs in: Preschool, www.networkedblogs.com/topic/preschool/

Web Sites

ABC Home Preschool, www.abchomepreschool.com/

Academy of Pediatrics, www.aap.org/

Child Care Education—Learning Through Play, www.squidoo.com/childrensnurseries

Child Development—Centers for Disease Control and Prevention, www.cdc.gov/ncbddd/child/preschoolers.htm

Early Childhood Education Made Easy, www.everythingpreschool.com/

Family Studies Laboratory, University of Waterloo, http://familystudies.uwaterloo.ca/main.html

First-School Preschool Activities and Crafts, www.first-school.ws/

Hanen Center, http://hanen.org

National Network for Child Care, www.nncc.org/Child.Dev/presch.dev.html

Parenting, www.parenthood.com/

PBS Kids, http://pbskids.org

Preschool Education, http://life.familyeducation.com/preschool/social-skills/41761.html

Preschool Outdoor Activities, www.education.com/activity/preschool/
outdoor/

Scholastic Parent and Child Magazine, www2.scholastic.com/browse/
parentsHome.jsp

Steps to Respect Program, the Committee for Children, www.cfchildren
.org/

National Organizations

American Academy of Child and Adolescent Psychiatry
3615 Wisconsin Avenue N.W.
Washington, D.C. 20016
202-966-7300

American Academy of Pediatrics
P.O. Box 927
Elk Grove Village, IL 60009
847-434-4000

American Speech-Language-Hearing Association
10801 Rockville Pike
Rockville, MD 20852
800-498-2071

Autism Speaks
New York
2 Park Avenue, 11th Floor
New York, NY 10016
212-252-8584

Federation for Children with Special Needs
1135 Tremont Street, Suite 420
Boston, MA 02120
617-236-7210

National Association for the Education of Young Children
1509 16th Street N.W.
Washington, D.C. 20036
800-424-2460

National Association of State Directors of Special Education
1800 Diagonal Road, Suite 320
Alexandria, VA, 22314
703-519-3800

National Safe Kids Campaign
1301 Pennsylvania Avenue N.W., Suite 1000
Washington D.C. 20004-1707
202-662-0600

Touchpoints Project
Children's Hospital, Boston
1295 Boylston Street, Suite 320
Boston, MA 02215
857-218-4451

United Cerebral Palsy Association
1660 L Street N.W.
Washington, D.C. 20036-56002
800-USA-5UCP

Zero to Three: The National Center for Infants, Toddlers, and Families
2000 M Street N.W.
Washington, D.C. 20036
202-638-1144

About the Authors

Ann Densmore, EdD, has appeared on the *Today Show* and was featured in the July 2008 edition of *Redbook* magazine. Her previous book, *Helping Children with Autism Become More Social* (2007), was chosen as Recommended Reading by *Choice* magazine.

Dr. Densmore has taught expressive language and social communication to hundreds of children for more than thirty years. As a speech pathologist, child psychologist, linguist, and audiologist, she has guided teachers, counseled staff members of hospitals and university medical centers, and lectured nationally and internationally on how to work with children. Perhaps more important than her professional qualifications is something her colleagues have long admired: her gift of being able to relate to and rescue the most isolated child. Her knowledge of these issues has made her a valuable consultant to the staffs of hospitals and university medical centers around the world.

Dr. Densmore received a grant from an international association, Autism Speaks, to develop a DVD, entitled, *Using Play to Foster Communication in Children with Autism and Asperger's Syndrome*. The film was supported by Autism Speaks with film production by FirstFrame, Inc. This product is for the lay audience as well as teachers and facilitators, and will be available in September 2010. Densmore was also the clinical advisor and a clinician in a video, *On the*

Spectrum: Children and Autism, produced by First Signs, an organization that distributed this video nationally to pediatricians who taught them how to treat children with autism.

Dr. Densmore has a doctorate in education with a specialty in child discourse from Clark University. She also has two master's degrees in communication disorders from California State University and in human development and psychology from Harvard University's Graduate School of Education. She is a certified speech and language pathologist and audiologist and a staff consultant for teachers. She is a frequent public speaker and does workshops for teachers/parents on play therapy for young children. For more information, visit her Web site at www.child-talk.com.

§

Margaret Bauman, MD, is an associate professor of neurology at Harvard Medical School, a neurologist and pediatrician at Massachusetts General Hospital, and an adjunct associate professor in the Department of Anatomy and Neurobiology at the Boston University School of Medicine. She is the founding director of LADDERS (Learning and Developmental Disabilities Evaluation and Rehabilitation Service), a satellite multidisciplinary clinic of the Department of Pediatrics of Massachusetts General Hospital. She is also the director of the Autism Research Foundation and the Autism Research Consortium in Boston, the child neurology consultant for Casa Colina Centers for Rehabilitation in Pomona, California, and the past medical director of the Autism Treatment Network. For more information, visit her Web site at www.ladders.org.

Dr. Bauman is an acclaimed pediatric neurologist. She has been interviewed on the *Today Show, NPR, BBC Television, CNBC, CNN,* and in the *New York Times, Time, Newsweek,* the *Huffington Post,* and the *Boston Globe,* among others. Dr. Bauman is the coauthor (with Dr. Thomas L. Kemper, MD) of *The Neurobiology of Autism* (1984).

About Harvard Medical School

SINCE 1782 HARVARD MEDICAL SCHOOL has been an international leader in the effort to improve health care and decrease human suffering from disease. Today more than ten thousand faculty members practice in seventeen affiliated hospitals and research institutions. Harvard Health Publications is the consumer health publishing division of Harvard Medical School and draws on the expertise of faculty members to translate the latest research in order to help individuals improve their health and quality of life.

For more information on Harvard Health Publications, go to health.harvard.edu.

Index